The Joy of Partnering with God

The Story of a Church That Did

By Will James
Senior Pastor

Paradise Valley Church
2727 E 7th St.
National City, CA 91950

www.FriendshipsForHope.org

TEACH Services, Inc.
P U B L I S H I N G
www.TEACHServices.com • (800) 367-1844

World rights reserved. This book or any portion thereof may not be copied or reproduced in any form or manner whatever, except as provided by law, without the written permission of the publisher, except by a reviewer who may quote brief passages in a review.

The author assumes full responsibility for the accuracy of all facts and quotations as cited in this book. The opinions expressed in this book are the author's personal views and interpretations, and do not necessarily reflect those of the publisher.

This book is provided with the understanding that the publisher is not engaged in giving spiritual, legal, medical, or other professional advice. If authoritative advice is needed, the reader should seek the counsel of a competent professional.

Copyright © 2016 Will James

Copyright © 2016 Teach Services, Inc.

ISBN-13: 978-1-4796-0732-7 (Paperback)

ISBN-13: 978-1-4796-0733-4 (ePub)

ISBN-13: 978-1-4796-0734-1 (Mobi)

Library of Congress Control Number: 2016916616

Unless otherwise marked, Scripture quotations are from the New International Version®, NIV®. Copyright ©1973, 1978, 1984, 2011 by Biblica, Inc.™ Used by permission. All rights reserved worldwide.

Scripture quotations marked CEV are from the Contemporary English Version, Second Edition, (CEV®) © 2006 American Bible Society. Used by permission. All rights reserved.

Scripture quotations marked CEB are taken from the Common English Bible®, CEB® Copyright © 2010, 2011 by Common English Bible™ Used by permission. All rights reserved worldwide.

Sections of this material first appeared in *Spectrum*, 2016, Vol. 44, No. 1. Used by permission.

Unless otherwise noted, all photos are by Jocelyn Fay.

Dedication

I dedicate this book to the memory of my mother, Arletia James, who all of her life impressed on me the reality that God had a special work He had created and prepared me for. It is because of her constant prayers and support that I have been at all successful in my ministry.

I also dedicate this book to the faithful members of the Paradise Valley Church, who have supported me and encouraged me to write a book on our shared journey in God's Word and in our partnership relationship with our God. Without you, there would be no story to share. Thank you for allowing me to take a sabbatical to have the time to write this book!

NOTE: The names in this book may have been changed or omitted to protect our students.

Table of Contents

Acknowledgements 9

Introduction 11

1. **Go** 13

2. **Surrender** 21

3. **Grow** 29

4. **Ask** 38

5. **Love** 47

6. **Choose** 55

7. **Bless** 64

8. **Give** 72

9. **Live** 80

10. Abide 87

The Story Continues on Our Ministry Web Page
www.FriendshipsForHope.org

Acknowledgements

Many people have made this book possible, for this is not *my* story; it is truly *our* story.

Members of the Paradise Valley Church, without you there would be no story.

Peggy James, my loving wife, you have always supported and believed in me and volunteered tirelessly with our team.

Staff and volunteer team, your support and lifting the load to give me time for this project is most appreciated!

Ephraim Bendantunguka, your passion for the refugees has inspired me.

Peter Thomas, your love for the Arabic community is contagious.

Our ESL Teachers, your love for our students is from God. Without you we wouldn't have a ministry to the refugees.

Jocelyn Fay, your encouragement and editorial assistance helped me as I wrote this manuscript.

Introduction

It has been a great privilege and honor to pastor the Paradise Valley Church in San Diego, California, for the past 14 years. During that time God has led us on a spiritual journey that has drawn us closer to Him, and also stretched us beyond our wildest dreams as we have partnered with God in ministry.

What God has accomplished through us is amazing, and I can hardly wait to see what else He has in store for us as we surrender ourselves to Him and faithfully follow His lead. I know that the story we share is only just the beginning.

It is my strong conviction that most Christians are living far below their potential when it comes to partnering with God. We will be spending considerable time studying together from the last words of Jesus to His disciples as recorded by Matthew and John. These are what Jesus felt were *the most important things* for them to remember as He was preparing to leave and return to heaven. In these passages Jesus pushes His disciples out of the nest, so to speak, encouraging them to grow with Him and allow Him to live within them and accomplish even more than He was able to do while He was on this earth. It is my prayer that this book will both inspire you and challenge you to a closer partnership with your God.

Pastor Will James, Author

Members of Paradise Valley Church, in National City, California, represent 62 countries of the world. At the church's colorful Festival of Nations in November many dress in their national costume, and one person from each country carries a flag down the center aisle to the front of the church.

Chapter 1
Go

Go and make disciples of all nations,
baptizing them in the name of the Father
and of the Son and of the Holy Spirit, and
teaching them to obey everything I have commanded you.
Matthew 28:19.

Let me ask you: Is there anything God cannot do? Is He all-powerful, all-knowing, and everywhere? Does He have angels who are much more powerful and capable than we are? Then why did He choose to use us to accomplish His mission on this earth?

Fourteen years ago, when I moved to San Diego to pastor the Paradise Valley Church, I found a church struggling to find its identity. It was a church, like many churches in North America, that had lost its reason for being, and many of the members were grappling with their own Christian identity.

This book is the story of a church that has begun to experience the transformative change that will happen when you consciously choose to enter a partnership type of relationship with Jesus, and allow Him to use you beyond your wildest dreams. In the process, the church has experienced the full meaning of Christ's words, "Do not let your heart be troubled" (John 14:1).

This book is the story of a church that has begun to experience the transformative change that will happen when you consciously choose to enter a partnership type of relationship with Jesus, and allow Him to use you beyond your wildest dreams.

This book will also help you to personalize the words of Christ and find peace and satisfaction when you accept God's invitation to "Go." And you will discover that together with Him, you can not only go but also find your greatest fulfillment in life as you do so.

Many have discovered that there is nothing like the thrill of knowing you are doing what God created you to do. When you discover your true purpose in life, and experience God working in and through you, you find such peace and fulfillment that you can understand why Jesus' final words to us just before returning to heaven were about partnering together with Him to accomplish the impossible.

Look at Jesus' final words as Matthew records them in Matthew 28:18–20: "Then Jesus came to them and said, 'All authority in heaven and on earth has been given to me. Therefore go and make disciples of all nations, baptizing them in the name of the Father and of the Son and of the Holy Spirit, and teaching them to obey everything I have commanded you. And surely I am with you always, to the very end of the age.'"

This text is familiar to most Christians, and it has stricken fear into many of our hearts. But I invite you to spend a few minutes with me looking at these last words of Christ before His ascension. They contain our marching orders. Jesus is telling us what He wants us to be doing.

Human nature seems to ask, "What must I do?" If we don't know what God wants us to do, we can easily get pulled aside, doing things that are not what He wants us to do.

Of course, the most important thing in life is to find Jesus. But I am assuming that if you are reading this book, you have found Jesus, and He is your Lord and Savior. So now that your salvation is secure, now that you

Chapter 1   Go

have accepted Jesus as your Lord and Savior and are living with the assurance of eternal life with Christ, what is your purpose in life here and now?

Jesus comes to us and says, "Go and make disciples of all nations, baptizing them in the name of the Father and of the Son and of the Holy Spirit, and teaching them to obey everything I have commanded you" (Matt. 28:19).

Can you do that? Or does the thought scare you? Let's try to unpack this command together and see if we can reduce the scare factor.

Jesus prefaced this command by saying, "All authority in heaven and on earth has been given to me" (verse 18).

Stop right there. Who has all the authority? Jesus. Why does He have it? He earned it. He was killed and placed in a tomb. He paid the price to defeat sin. Because of what He has done, His Father—and *our* Father—has given to Him all authority in heaven and on earth.

Then Jesus adds the large word "therefore," or "because." "Because all authority has been given to Me," He says, "I have authority over you, and I am saying to you, 'Go and make disciples of all nations, baptizing them in the name of the Father and of the Son and of the Holy Spirit, and teaching them to obey everything I have commanded you.'"

Notice, this is not an optional request. I ask you again, does it scare you? Is it something you can do? Is Jesus going to command you to do something you are unable to do? *Yes!* Jesus *always* asks us to do the impossible. If He didn't ask us to do what is humanly impossible, we wouldn't need to partner with Him. For us on our own, this *is* an impossible task!

But Jesus doesn't stop after giving us this impossible task. He reassures us, "Surely I am with you always, to the very end of the age" (verse 20).

Jesus is saying, "I want to partner with you to accomplish what I have called you to do. I want to go with you." If Jesus is with you, and He is living in you, is it possible to do what He asks you to do? Yes, it is!

I am very proud of the members of the Paradise Valley Church, because we are beginning to accomplish the impossible together with Jesus. I say "beginning," because we won't be finished until the "end of the age," which will be when Jesus returns. And I do not think we have begun to experience the fullness of what Jesus wants to do in and through us. As we go, we are beginning, together with Him, to accomplish some of what He wants to see done in sharing the everlasting gospel to the ends of this earth.

Does this mean that we all get up and preach the everlasting gospel from the pulpit or on the street corner? No, not at all. That is not what the text is saying. It says, "Go and make disciples of all nations." We are to go to where the people are and make disciples—people who follow their Master. It is to demonstrate to others what it means to partner together with our Master, Jesus Christ.

Parents: God wants to live in you, and by your life and example to share the love of Jesus with your children in your home. To teach them everything you know about the God who loves you and loves them.

Young people: God wants to go with you into your classroom at school and use you to touch the lives of your teachers and classmates, sharing with them by your life and example what it is like to be a child of God.

At your job: God wants to go with you, and through your life to influence your boss and coworkers with the truths about a God who loves them. A God whose Son came to pay the penalty for their sins and to give them the opportunity to have a future and an eternal life with Him.

As God lives in your life and mine, He will reveal to us daily the things He wants us to take care of. He will bring people into contact with us, divine appointments at which He wants us to meet a need, say a word of encouragement, or give some godly counsel. We need to be open and to watch for these divine appointments God is leading us to.

As God lives in your life and mine, He will reveal to us daily the things He wants us to take care of. He will bring people into contact with us, divine appointments at which He wants us to meet a need, say a word of encouragement, or give some godly counsel. We need to be open and to watch for these divine appointments God is leading us to.

In 2008 I experienced one of these divine appointments—with a man named Ephraim Bendantunguka. When I met him, little did I know how much my life would change!

Ephraim was born in what is now the Democratic Republic of Congo, graduated from Mudende, a French-speaking Christian university in Rwanda (destroyed during the genocide there), and pastored a

Chapter 1 Go   17

5,000-member church in Kigali, Rwanda's capital city. In 1992 he went with his family to Germany to get his master's degree.

When the genocide broke out back home six months after their departure, Ephraim and his family became refugees in Germany. After earning his systematic theology degree, Ephraim discovered that job opportunities for him were limited. He worked as an assistant nurse in a retirement home, then, with his wife, Regine, assisted immigrants and refugees before coming to America to try to provide a better life for his family.

A friend from Rwanda urged Ephraim to move to San Diego. When he did, he tried calling local churches to ask for temporary housing. That Friday afternoon he finally reached a church secretary at Paradise Valley who was able to help him, and soon he and his family were camping in the Community Services Center of my church. This is where I met them when I returned from a trip to Manila.

The arrival of Ephraim Bendantunguka and his wife, Regine Nyirakanyana, refugees from Germany, was the beginning of Paradise Valley Church's assimilation project for other refugees in San Diego County. In its five years of existence it has bettered the lives of hundreds of refugees, many of whom have found jobs or are studying for new careers.

The recession started about that same time, and I felt God impressing me that we should do something about the need for food for people in our community. I have been preaching for years, "If God shows you a need, it is because He wants you to meet that need; and if you will step out in faith to meet that need, God will supply the resources to do so." Little did I know how God was going to test and strengthen my beliefs!

I advertised on Craigslist that we were looking for a walk-in cooler. The first to respond was a company that installed them. They said, "If you get a cooler, let us know and we will go and dismantle it and install it on your property free of cost."

The next week I got a call from a florist who was going out of business. She said, "I have a large walk-in cooler you can have."

The next year we collected and gave away more than 1,000 pounds of food each week and thought we were busy. But we had only just begun! By this time Ephraim and his family had become members of Paradise Valley Church. Ephraim played a major role in the expansion of this food ministry into what has become Friendships for Hope, an assimilation project for refugees like him and his family in San Diego. We will get better acquainted with Ephraim and his family in future chapters.

I've grown from pastoring a good church to what is now a great church. My job description has changed dramatically as well. Not only that, but God has provided, and we have spent more than $1 million in the past five years in our ministry to our community.

We are discovering together what Jesus' final words to us really are all about. Jesus' final conversation with His followers, according to the apostle John, starts in John 14. Jesus is talking to His followers as they walk to the Garden of Gethsemane, where He knows He is going to be arrested and ultimately killed. Yet in spite of this knowledge, notice what He says to them, and in turn to us, because although He was physically talking to the eleven disciples, His words are still true for all of His followers today.

Jesus says, "Do not let your hearts be troubled. You believe in God; believe also in me. My Father's house has many rooms; if that were not so, would I have told you that I am going there to prepare a place for you? And if I go and prepare a place for you, I will come back and take you to be with me that you also may be where I am" (verses 1–3).

These are probably the best loved and most often memorized verses in the entire Bible, but notice the context of these verses.

The disciples are on the verge of the most terrifying days of their lives. They are going to watch Jesus being crucified and their dreams being crushed. Yet Jesus tells them, "Do not let your hearts be troubled."

Jesus is on His way to pay the price to make it possible for us to go to that heavenly home. He knows who He is, and He also knows who His Father is. Yet He says to His friends, "Do not let your hearts be troubled."

He could say that because He saw the big picture. He knew there was more beyond. Yes, He was going to die, but that would not be the end of the story.

Notice how Jesus describes for us the partnership He has with His Father God in verses 10 and 11: "Don't you believe that I am in the Father,

Chapter 1   Go

and that the Father is in me? The words I say to you I do not speak on my own authority. Rather, it is the Father, living in me, who is doing his work. Believe me when I say that I am in the Father and the Father is in me; or at least believe on the evidence of the works themselves."

Here Jesus describes for us how He lived His life while on this earth. It was in a partnership with His Father. He invites us to look at it and let the evidence speak for itself.

And then, here in John's account of the last words of Jesus, we read more about the partnership Jesus wants to have with us.

"Whoever believes in me will do the works I have been doing, and they will do even greater things than these, because I am going to the Father. And I will do whatever you ask in my name, so that the Father may be glorified in the Son. You may ask me for anything in my name, and I will do it" (verses 12–14).

Jesus wants to live and dwell in you in the same way that His Father lived and dwelled in Him while He was here on this earth, "so that the Father may be glorified in the Son."

Jesus says, "Look at all the things I did: healing the sick, raising the dead, turning water to wine, multiplying the few loaves and fishes to feed more than 5,000 people. But you will do even greater things than these because I am going to my Father, and I am going to live in you so that the Father may be glorified in the Son."

And don't miss the last sentence: "You may ask me for anything in my name, and I will do it" (verse 14). Who will do it? Jesus says, "I will."

It is not for our glory; it is not even for Jesus' glory. It is for the glory of God the Father. Jesus wants us to be in a living partnership with Him so that we can bring glory to God the Father in all that He does through us.

Here at Paradise Valley Church, we have only just begun. Jesus has much greater things He wants to do through us as we partner with Him, but it is to bring glory to our Father God that He wants to do this.

All authority in heaven and on earth has been given to Jesus. Only as we submit ourselves to that authority can we even hope to accomplish all that He asks us to do, for without Him, we can do nothing.

This book is intended to explore what a partnership with Jesus looks like. It is not intended to bring glory to the Paradise Valley Church, although I will be sharing our story in the process. It is all about what God is doing in and through the members of this church as we attempt to live in this partnership with our God.

I asked at the beginning of this chapter, "Why did Jesus choose to use us to accomplish His work instead of doing it Himself or having angels do it?" I believe the answer has something to do with His wanting to take people who are incapable of doing anything themselves, and in a partnership with them accomplish the impossible for God's glory.

Are you ready to explore a partnership with Jesus, and in the process bring glory and honor to your Father God? Are you ready to do the impossible together with the God of possibilities? Oh yes—and also to experience peace for your troubled heart?

Chapter 2
Surrender

Surrender to God! Resist the devil,
and he will run from you. Come near to God,
and he will come near to you. Clean up your lives, you sinners.
Purify your hearts, you people who can't make up your mind.
James 4:7, 8, CEV.

The subject of this chapter is one we often try to avoid, but I hope to help you to embrace it. It is hard to surrender because we are all broken, and broken people are insecure and usually try to keep control of everything in their life. To surrender means that we are releasing our authority and our hold and letting go. That is extremely difficult for broken people. Everyone reading this book is imperfect, and none of us is damaged in the same way. Our brokenness is as unique as we are, and yet it still makes it extremely difficult to surrender to God.

None of us can look at another and think, *"They are broken, but I am not."* The Scriptures speak of our condition: "All have sinned and fall short of the glory of God" (Rom. 3:23).

Many times in our brokenness we misunderstand one another and are hurt in the process, which often makes us all the more broken.

It is important for us to recognize our own brokenness, our own weaknesses, because until we do, we will not feel our need of God, and more important, we will not surrender ourselves to Him.

It is important for us to recognize our own brokenness, our own weaknesses, because until we do, we will not feel our need of God, and more important, we will not surrender ourselves to Him. As long as we feel confident of our own abilities and feel that we can handle everything, we won't submit to God. And if we don't surrender to God, we will never partner together with Him, and we will never receive the gift of His healing touch and empowerment in our life.

Further, until we recognize our own limitations we won't recognize that we need one another. It is difficult to accomplish anything of real value by ourselves. Oh, we often hear of the "self-made man," but the reality of life is that we, by ourselves, are incapable of any greatness. We need someone to come alongside of us and join with us if we are ever going to achieve anything of real value.

Stop and think about it a minute. Could that be one of the reasons Jesus established the church?

- How many missionaries could you send … by yourself?
- How many countries could you go to and spread the gospel … by yourself?
- How many languages could you translate the Bible into … by yourself?
- How many churches could you build … by yourself?
- How many people could you feed … by yourself?

It always takes more than one to accomplish anything of any size or importance. A committee of one is pretty useless.

But let's get back to our brokenness. Until we recognize our condition we will never search for the solution.

As we look at the Scriptures, we don't have to look very far before we realize that everywhere we look we see broken people—prophets, kings,

Chapter 2   Surrender

apostles—everyone. But the wonderful story of the Bible is that God takes these imperfect people and uses them to accomplish great things.

One story stands out in my mind because it illustrates something I need for myself. It's the story of the life and example of perhaps the greatest leader who ever lived—Moses.

When we look closely at Moses, we discover that he was broken, too. Taken away from his own mother at an early age, he was raised in the palace of Egypt as an adopted son of Pharaoh's daughter. We see him struggling with surrendering to God.

Missing his own family, finally one day in desperation he murdered one of the Egyptian taskmasters who was beating one of his relatives. He had to flee for his own life. He spent the next forty years watching sheep in the hot Midian desert, broken. In fact, when God comes to him after those forty years with the sheep, that's what he tells God: "Who am I that I should go to Pharaoh and bring the Israelites out of Egypt?" (Exod. 3:11).

God tells Moses what He wants him to do, and gives him signs and wonders, yet Moses is hesitant, because he knows he is inadequate. He says to God, "Pardon your servant, Lord. I have never been eloquent, neither in the past nor since you have spoken to your servant. I am slow of speech and tongue" (Exod. 4:10).

Oh, how I relate to Moses! I also am slow of speech and tongue. I stuttered growing up and found it much easier not to talk at all, yet I felt the call of God early in my life to be a pastor. Everyone told me I didn't have the necessary skills. In fact, when I took an aptitude test in high school, it said I should be a mechanic. I was broken, and like Moses, I recognized my brokenness, which is not a bad thing to do. Like Moses, I said to God, "I don't have the necessary skills to do what You are asking me to do."

Like Moses, I said to God, "I don't have the necessary skills to do what You are asking me to do."

God answered me as He answered Moses: "Who gave human beings their mouths? Who makes them deaf or mute? Who gives them sight or makes them blind? Is it not I, the Lord? Now go; I will help you speak and will teach you what to say" (verses 11, 12).

God didn't deny that Moses and I were broken, but He told us, "I am able to heal any brokenness. Just trust Me and do what I am asking you to do." Yes, I relate well to Moses, and that is why I love his story!

Even after reassurance from God, Moses still hesitated. He was no different than you and me. We don't like to step out of our comfort zones and do things we have never done or think we can't do. As Moses did, we ask God, "Please send someone else" (verse 13). Still struggling with surrender, Moses said, "Let someone else do it."

Notice carefully God's reply. "Then the Lord's anger burned against Moses and he said, 'What about your brother, Aaron the Levite? I know he can speak well. He is already on his way to meet you, and he will be glad to see you. You shall speak to him and put words in his mouth; I will help both of you speak and will teach you what to do. He will speak to the people for you, and it will be as if he were your mouth and as if you were God to him. But take this staff in your hand so you can perform the signs with it'" (verses 14–17).

Have you ever made God angry? Have you ever said no to something you know God has asked you to do? Probably very few of us have had a conversation with God in the same way that Moses did, but if we are listening, God does often speak to us.

God speaks to us through His Word, the Bible; through other Christians; and yes, He speaks to us with impressions and in direct answers to our prayers. He still wants to communicate His will to us. Don't ever believe that God has stopped talking to us.

If we will obey God, He will lead and direct our lives. If we are listening, we will know when God speaks to us. And we will know what He wants us to do. It will often be the case, as it was with Moses, that what He asks of us is beyond what we think we are capable of doing. If what God asks us to do were not beyond our own abilities, we wouldn't need to partner with Him, which He wants us to do.

I am thankful that even though Moses made God angry, God didn't give up on him. He didn't give up on me, and He won't give up on you. God has promised us that He will never leave us nor forsake us. Don't take my word for it, let's read it! "Never will I leave you; never will I forsake you" (Heb. 13:5).

Isn't that good news? Even when we rebel and make God angry, as Moses did, He will not abandon us.

Moses surrendered and went where God asked him to go, and the rest of the story is that God used Moses in miraculous ways. Moses led the

Chapter 2   Surrender   25

children of Israel out of Egypt and led them for the next forty years in the same wilderness where he had herded sheep for his father-in-law.

Was it easy? No, Moses many times felt the task was too much for him and questioned God, but God continued to lead him and use him on that long journey to their new home.

God specializes in taking broken people and using them to accomplish great things for Him.

God specializes in taking broken people and using them to accomplish great things for Him. One word of caution: we are all broken people, so don't expect perfection from human leaders. If we expect perfection, we will be disappointed when in their brokenness they let us down. Only God is perfect. We need to keep our eyes on God, not on broken leaders.

This happened even in Moses' life. One day he became frustrated with the people. Now, to be honest, who could blame him after all he had done for them? It wasn't easy leading this rebellious bunch of former slaves from Egypt to the Promised Land.

They came to him complaining ... again. Moses responded in frustration in his brokenness. Look at the story in Numbers 20:2–15. It begins, "Now there was no water for the community, and the people gathered in opposition to Moses and Aaron. They quarreled with Moses and said, 'If only we had died when our brothers fell dead before the Lord! Why did you bring the Lord's community into this wilderness, that we and our livestock should die here? Why did you bring us up out of Egypt to this terrible place? It has no grain or figs, grapevines or pomegranates. And there is no water to drink!'" (verses 2–5).

It had been nearly forty years since they left Egypt, and God had provided for them again and again, yet here they were complaining to Moses ... again.

Reading on: "The Lord said to Moses, 'Take the staff, and you and your brother Aaron gather the assembly together. Speak to that rock before their eyes and it will pour out its water. You will bring water out of the rock for the community so they and their livestock can drink'" (verses 7, 8).

Could Moses bring water out of a rock? No, but God wanted to partner with Moses to provide water for the people's needs. God told Moses to speak to the rock, and it would pour out water.

That rock represented God, the supplier of all our needs. God told Moses to speak to the rock (Him), and the rock (He) would pour out water.

But what did Moses do in his brokenness and frustration? "Moses took the staff from the Lord's presence, just as he commanded him. He and Aaron gathered the assembly together in front of the rock and Moses said to them, 'Listen, you rebels, must we bring you water out of this rock?' Then Moses raised his arm and struck the rock twice with his staff. Water gushed out, and the community and their livestock drank" (verses 9–11).

Here is a beautiful example of God not forsaking or leaving Moses. Moses didn't do what God asked him to do, he didn't surrender, yet God still honored Moses before the people. God still gave the water to the people.

Have you ever become frustrated in your responsibilities at home or at work? God still wants to partner with you to accomplish what He has asked you to do.

Yes, the job is too much for us. Many of us face horrendous challenges in our lives. The only way we can ever make it through those challenges is to partner together with God.

Will we make mistakes? Yes. There will be times when in our brokenness we refuse to surrender. But God still says, "Never will I leave you; never will I forsake you" (Heb. 13:5).

God has proven true to us in our partnership ministry with Him at Paradise Valley Church. Challenges face us almost every day in our ministries here. We know what frustration feels like. But we also have known the joy of surrendering those frustrations to God and watching Him work things out. He is with us!

There are so many needs facing our refugee families. Their limited income just can't stretch to meet all their needs. Food stamps won't buy such essentials as soap, toilet paper, and hygiene items. We are constantly looking for ways to provide these items for them. One day my wife, Peggy, was on her way to the church. She prayed as she drove, telling God of the need for forty containers of laundry soap. Soon after she arrived at the church, one of our volunteers drove in with a pickup full of laundry soap. Someone had vandalized a store by opening a bottle of soap and pouring it over all of the other bottles of soap on the shelf. The store had given all the soap-coated bottles to us. God has so many ways to provide for us! We can only thank Him and praise His name.

As our activities have expanded and we have needed volunteers to accomplish more and more tasks, God has brought us just the right people when we needed them. And after Ephraim and his family, about whom we wrote in Chapter 1, experienced setback after setback in their efforts to

Chapter 2 Surrender

obtain permanent resident status in the United States, we wondered why God wasn't answering our prayers. But He was, and we gave Him thanks on that happy day when their green cards arrived.

Finances have been a challenge as well. Continually financing our community services and our assistance to refugees is way too much for us to accomplish on our own. We are daily being reminded that God is in charge, and we must keep our eyes focused on Him. We are asking Him to lead us as we look for business opportunities to be training sites for refugees as well as a revenue stream to support our work with them.

We are moving that direction. In 2015 our rummage sales and thrift store generated more than $75,000 toward our ministry budget of $350,000. Obviously we are not there yet, but that is close to a quarter of our budget, and we are certain God will continue to open doors for us. And yes, during the past five years we have spent more than $1 million in our ministry! God has opened the windows of heaven and supplied our needs. We have very little money in the bank, but that is not where God has told us to keep it. We are busy storing up treasures in heaven in the lives of the precious people He has called us to minister to.

Income from two rummage sales a year helps support Community Services projects. Volunteers spend hundreds of hours processing and pricing donated items from individuals and estate sales and setting up for the massive three-day event.

We have taught and empowered more than 100 refugee families to move on with college education or to find jobs and get off the welfare system that supported them when the United Nations resettled them in San Diego. We are working with another ninety-five families in all stages of growth toward self-sufficiency. Some of them are struggling with learning English, but many more are either looking for job opportunities or completing their education to become plumbers, nurses, and caregivers.

We are discovering that even in our brokenness, we find that God is there, and nothing is impossible for Him to bring us through. We are constantly being reminded of what Jesus tells us: "I am the vine; you are the branches. If you remain in me and I in you, you will bear much fruit; apart from me you can do nothing. If you do not remain in me, you are like a branch that is thrown away and withers; such branches are picked up, thrown into the fire and burned. If you remain in me and my words remain in you, ask whatever you wish, and it will be done for you. This is to my Father's glory, that you bear much fruit, showing yourselves to be my disciples" (John 15:5–8).

We are inadequate and flawed, but if we will daily surrender and partner with God, if we will stay connected to Him, there is nothing we cannot accomplish. It is not for our glory, but it is all for the glory of our Father God.

Don't look at your brokenness or dwell on someone else's. Keep your eyes focused on God, stay surrendered and connected to Him, and allow Him to use you for His glory today.

The opening of P. V. Thrift Store coincided with the opening of English language classes on November 6, 2011. The store provides work for refugees along with countless opportunities for them to practice speaking English with customers.

Chapter 3
Grow

Like newborn babies, crave pure spiritual milk,
so that by it you may grow up in your salvation,
now that you have tasted that the Lord is good.
1 Peter 2: 2, 3.

In Chapter 1 I asked, "Why did God choose to use us to accomplish His mission on this earth? Why, when He is all-powerful, and there is nothing He couldn't do by Himself or use His mighty angels to accomplish, did He choose to use weak human beings to carry out His purposes?"

Why did God, when He is all-powerful, and there is nothing He couldn't do by Himself or use His mighty angels to accomplish, did He choose to use weak human beings to carry out His purposes?

The conclusion was that the answer must lie somewhere in the realm of His wanting to take someone incapable of doing anything alone and in partnership with them accomplish the impossible for God's glory.

This is exactly what I see happening here at Paradise Valley. As we faithfully grow in our partnership with God, we see Him opening doors and leading us down paths we never would have dreamed of taking. We are giving away an average of 10,000 pounds of food and more than 400 pieces of clothing to about 400 families in our community each week. (And we thought we were busy when giving away 1,000 pounds of food a week!)

Jesus promised that "whoever believes in me will do the works I have been doing, and they will do even greater things than these, because I am going to the Father. And I will do whatever you ask in my name, so that the Father may be glorified in the Son. You may ask me for anything in my name, and I will do it" (John 14:12–14).

Let's spend some more time on this promise and on what it means to us. Here Jesus describes for us the ideal partnership, one so powerful that He says we will be able to do even more than He did when He was here on this earth.

What does this look like? What will happen when we are in this kind of partnership with Jesus? Will it free us of worries and troubles? Will everything be easy?

Let's look at a biblical example of partnership, which the apostle Paul describes when he writes about the church in Thessalonica: "We ought always to thank God for you, brothers and sisters, and rightly so, because your faith is growing more and more, and the love all of you have for one another is increasing. Therefore, among God's churches we boast about your perseverance and faith in all the persecutions and trials you are enduring. All this is evidence that God's judgment is right, and as a result you will be counted worthy of the kingdom of God, for which you are suffering. God is just: He will pay back trouble to those who trouble you and give relief to you who are troubled, and to us as well. This will happen when the Lord Jesus is revealed from heaven in blazing fire with his powerful angels" (2 Thess. 1:3–7).

Here is a church in the New Testament that has Jesus' promise and invitation to partner together with Him. Notice how it is happening. Paul says in verse 4, "Among God's churches we boast about your perseverance and faith in all the persecutions and trials you are enduring."

Right up front I want to do away with the myth that partnering with Jesus means that you won't have any trials or troubles. That just isn't so. But what it does mean is that Jesus is with us through the trials and trou-

Chapter 3   Grow

bles, and He is using the adversity in our life to help us *grow* into all that He wants us to be. If Jesus is with you, will you be able to make it through? Yes!

Trials and troubles do not mean you are doing something wrong, or that God is not with you. In fact, they mean just the opposite—you are doing something right! Paul says he boasts that the Thessalonians are persevering and *growing* in faith through all their trials and troubles.

All too often I see Christians who have faced a difficult time in their life and lost their faith, wandering off discouraged and thinking God must have abandoned them. A great text for you to use the next time you face one of these difficult times comes from James, the brother of Jesus: "Consider it pure joy, my brothers and sisters, whenever you face trials of many kinds, because you know that the testing of your faith produces perseverance. Let perseverance finish its work so that you may be mature and complete, not lacking anything" (James 1:2–4).

Now, don't read this wrong! This is *not* saying that God is bringing you the trials! God does *not* bring you trials. It is the enemy of God who brings them. Satan is trying to discourage you and get you to turn against God. But God's promise is that when Satan brings adversity, Jesus walks with us through it and helps us grow and come out stronger on the other end.

Probably few people understand this better than the refugees our church serves. One of them is Jean-Marie, a college graduate and former math and French teacher. He came to the United States because of the trials he faced in his homeland, the Democratic Republic of Congo. He is a survivor of his first wife's murder and several prison terms in the Congo and Rwanda.

One day in Nairobi, Kenya, where he and his second wife, Sudi, had established a new life, the Office of the United Nations High Commissioner for Refugees informed him that his life was in danger.

Jean-Marie spoke several languages when the United Nations settled him and his family in San Diego, but none of those languages was English. A quick learner, he soon became fluent enough in English to work at P. V. Thrift store. He was assistant manager there before transferring to a full-time job at nearby Paradise Valley Hospital.

The people who had murdered his first wife knew where he was and were coming after him. The United Nations put him in protective custody and began paperwork for his evacuation to America.

Jean-Marie, Sudi, and their four children arrived in San Diego in July 2011. Although he spoke French, Swahili, and Lingala, he knew no English.

At home in his apartment one day, he looked out the window and saw Ephraim Bendantunguka, our Refugee Assimilation Project director, distributing food to other refugees in the apartment complex. He went out and learned that Ephraim also spoke French. Ephraim told him that he would return the next day and take Jean-Marie to church.

"I went by myself and saw it was interesting. I came the next week with my family. After three months I started to learn about the Bible and Christianity," he said. Soon he, Sudi, and their children were baptized.

After learning English at our English language school, Jean-Marie worked at our P. V. Thrift Store for more than two years. Now he works full time in environmental services at the Paradise Valley Hospital. His family story also has turned out well. Jean-Marie and Sudi's youngest son, John Jack, was born in 2013, and three older children from Jean-Marie's previous marriage, who had remained in Africa, joined the family last year. They also have been baptized.

Through a church that Jean-Marie describes as "very helpful to all the refugees," Jean Marie is learning that Christianity is about growing and maturing in Christ. In spite of his trials and tribulations, he knows that God was with him then and is with him all the time.

I love what the prophet Isaiah says about hardships: "This is what the Lord says—he who created you, Jacob, he who formed you, Israel: 'Do not fear, for I have redeemed you; I have summoned you by name; you are mine'" (Isa. 43:1).

Who is speaking? The Lord—the God who formed and created us. And He says, "Do not fear, for I have redeemed you; I have summoned you by name; you are mine."

Right after He tells us not to fear, that we belong to Him, He gives us further encouragement: "When you pass through the waters, I will be with you; and when you pass through the rivers, they will not sweep over you. When you walk through the fire, you will not be burned; the flames will not set you ablaze. For I am the Lord your God, the Holy One of Israel, your Savior" (Isa. 43:2, 3).

Chapter 3   Grow

Notice, it does not say *if*; it says *when* … and when these things happen we are to remember that the God who created and formed us and called us by name still says, "Do not be afraid, for I am with you."

This is the same promise Jesus made as He was walking with His disciples to the Garden of Gethsemane: "Do not let your hearts be troubled. You believe in God; believe also in me. My Father's house has many rooms; if that were not so, would I have told you that I am going there to prepare a place for you? And if I go and prepare a place for you, I will come back and take you to be with me that you also may be where I am" (John 14:1–3).

But reading that and believing it can be two different things. When we are going through difficulties, it can be hard to remember that Jesus is with us. But each time we come through a trial, we come out the other end with a stronger faith in God. So even though Satan is trying to defeat us, what God is really doing is building us and maturing us as we make it through with Jesus.

It is as Jesus' brother James writes, "The testing of your faith produces perseverance. Let perseverance finish its work so that you may be mature and complete, not lacking anything" (James 1:3, 4).

Parents, you all know this is true. As you raise your children, you must allow them to struggle and try to accomplish the difficult things in life or they will never mature and become strong. If you do everything for them and don't let them stretch and grow—and yes, even make mistakes—they will stay weak and small and ultimately fail in life.

Our Heavenly Father, as well, must allow us to face the troubles and trials of life so that we will grow and mature. But He has promised to be there in the trials with us. Our spiritual life is all about learning to trust God. This will happen only through experience. As we trust Him with the small things of life and find Him to be trustworthy, we will grow until we are able to trust Him with the really big issues of life as well.

> *Our spiritual life is all about learning to trust God.*

Solomon, the wisest king of Israel, says it this way: "Trust in the Lord with all your heart and lean not on your own understanding; in all your ways submit to him, and he will make your paths straight" (Prov. 3:5, 6).

Every relationship is based on trust, or the lack thereof. As you get to know a person, you either learn to trust them or not to trust them. It is the defining element in every relationship in life. If someone proves to be trustworthy, it is not difficult to learn to trust them. However, if someone proves to be untrustworthy, it would be crazy to trust them, because you will be hurt in the process.

God says: "Do not fear, for I am with you; do not be dismayed, for I am your God. I will strengthen you and help you; I will uphold you with my righteous right hand" (Isa. 41:10). You will be able to do that only when you know personally that God is trustworthy. You cannot take my word for it. Trust can come only from a personal relationship with your God.

The psalmist invites us to "taste and see that the Lord is good; blessed is the one who takes refuge in him. Fear the Lord, you his holy people, for those who fear him lack nothing" (Ps. 34:8, 9).

That word *fear* does not mean to be afraid of God, but to honor Him. Let's read that again from a modern translation, The Common English Bible, and see if it makes more sense. "Taste and see how good the Lord is! The one who takes refuge in him is truly happy! You who are the Lord's holy ones, honor him, because those who honor him don't lack a thing."

We are not literally tasting or eating Jesus; we are putting Him to the test and learning to reverence and trust Him as He proves trustworthy. We must trust God if we are going to really grow in our partnership with Him. We must literally put Him and His promises to us to the test. We must see *if* He will really do all that He says He will do.

Here at Paradise Valley Church, with our ministry for refugees, we have been experiencing this partnership with God. From our food ministry we began to become aware of pockets of refugees in our community. A refugee is someone who has had to flee their homeland because of war, persecution, or disaster, and the United Nations works with them to relocate them to a new home. They come as legal residents of the country they are assigned to, and usually have government support finan-

Every Tuesday, Thongsouay loads his car with bags of groceries to deliver to families in a community of Laotian refugees. After he added several Bhutanese families in the same neighborhood to his weekly delivery list, the Bhutanese began attending Paradise Valley Church. They formed the nucleus of the first class of English learners.

Chapter 3 Grow

cially for a short period of time until they can get a job and begin to support themselves.

One of our local elders, Thongsouay Sakdarak, was a Buddhist monk of the highest order in Laos. During the Vietnam War he became a refugee and was converted to Christianity in his camp. God used him to help convert more than a thousand Laotians to Christianity while still in the refugee camp. Here in San Diego, he began taking some of our food to a group of Laotian refugees each week. In the same apartment complex where the Laotian refugees lived were a group of Bhutanese refugees who had lived in squalor in the refugee camps of Nepal for fifteen years. They saw the food coming each week and finally asked if Thongsouay would bring them some. He agreed and soon was delivering food to more than sixty families a week.

Soon these refugees wanted to come to church, but we did not speak their language, and they did not speak ours. Besides, how would we get them to church? We borrowed a bus from the church that was renting our fellowship hall each weekend. This was the beginning of our busing ministry. We now own two buses and send them out each Sabbath morning to bring busloads of refugees to church.

Ephraim, with his experience working with immigrants and refugees in Germany, became alive as these events were happening. He began telling me we needed to start a ministry to assimilate refugees into American society.

I said, "How can we afford to start a school for refugees?"

He remembered what he'd heard me say many times and turned my words back on me: "If God shows you a need, it is

Paradise Valley Church owns two buses, at least one of which is on the road six days a week. With their volunteer drivers, two buses bring refugees to church and take them home again on Sabbaths. Their buses' other primary function is bringing refugee students on weekdays to ESL classes and their children to school at San Diego Academy, a K-12 school.

because He wants you to do something about that need, remember, Pastor?"

We began to think and pray about what God was showing us and what He wanted us to do. Knowing that before refugees could get jobs they needed to learn basic English language skills, we began to explore how we could teach English to our Bhutanese refugee friends. We soon learned that in order for them to get their food stamps, housing allowance, and medical insurance they must either attend language classes or volunteer to learn a job skill for a minimum of thirty-five hours a week. We formulated a plan and submitted it to the San Diego County. Soon the county certified us to offer the hours for ESL (English as a Second Language) classes and work experience. Our ministry to refugees had begun, with Ephraim as our director and about twenty students he had recruited from several apartment complexes.

It has been a series of stepping through doors as God has opened them, and yes, He has provided for all of our needs as we have faithfully done what He has asked us to do. Our faith has been stretched—there has never been more than enough, but just enough. It is proving to be a stretching, growing experience, but we are learning that God is faithful, and He is walking with us through all the trials of beginning this ministry.

That trial you are facing today—or are going to face tomorrow—was not brought to you by God. But He has promised to be with you through it and help you to grow and mature in your Christian walk as you find Him to be trustworthy. As you grow and mature in your Christian experience, God will be able to trust you with the power and ability to accomplish greater things together with Him for His glory.

There is no shortcut to maturity. We all know that children are not born mature. Maturity comes through experience. It comes by facing challenges and overcoming, by growing through the experiences of life. Becoming a mature Christian also comes through experience. As we learn that God is always there, and that He walks with us through all our troubles and brings us out stronger on the other side, then we mature as Christians. Just as we cannot trust our 10-year-old with the car, God cannot trust us with everything until we have grown and matured.

If we want to experience the fulfillment of Jesus' promise, "Whoever believes in me will do the works I have been doing, and they will do even greater things than these" (John 14:12), then we must grow to where we truly believe in Jesus.

Chapter 3   Grow

To do this, we must be spending time with Him daily. We must be consciously submitting ourselves to Him and allowing Him to live and dwell within us.

We must be spending time with Him daily.
We must be consciously submitting ourselves
to Him and allowing Him to live
and dwell within us.

I invite you to spend time each morning renewing that relationship with God. Invite Him to enter your life and guide you throughout your entire day. In the process, may you feel His arms of love around you and hear His voice quietly saying, "This is the way."

It is rewarding to see the members of our church growing closer to God as we are experiencing Him walking and talking with us in our ministry with Him. We are learning from experience that it is true that He will never leave us nor forsake us. We are discovering that the setbacks we all face in life are not brought to us by God, but that He certainly uses these events to get our attention and to teach us that He is always there for us, helping us make it through.

It is exciting to see that our refugee friends are learning this from us, as they see us turning to God and asking Him what He wants us to do. This is what the next chapter is all about.

Chapter 4
Ask

Ask and it will be given to you; seek and you will find;
knock and the door will be opened to you.
Matthew 7:7.

We have seen that God wants to partner with us to continue the work that Christ began when He was here on earth. He has chosen to work in and through us to do even greater things than He did.

It's obvious that we don't have much to bring to this partnership, because we are incapable of doing what He has asked us to accomplish. We can do our task only by allowing God to empower and use us. Jesus told us, "Without me ye can do nothing" (John 15:5, KJV).

We have seen how important it is for God to grow and mature us so that we will give Him the glory for what He accomplishes through us. It is not what we are able to do, but rather what He is doing through us; therefore, the glory belongs to God.

We are using the last words of Jesus as recorded by Matthew and John as our marching orders for this book. Let's review them.

In Matthew 28:19 we learn that we are to "go and make disciples of all nations," and in verse 20 we are reassured that as we do that, Jesus will always be with us. Along with this are Jesus' words to His followers on the

Chapter 4   Ask

way to the Garden of Gethsemane, "Whoever believes in me will do the works I have been doing, and they will do even greater things than these, because I am going to the Father. And I will do whatever you ask in my name, so that the Father may be glorified in the Son. You may ask me for anything in my name, and I will do it" (John 14:12–14).

Now, a word of caution here. Some people take verse 14 out of context. They say you can literally ask Him for *anything* you want and Jesus must give it to you.

Is that really what the text is saying? *No!* Keep it in context. Jesus is talking about partnering with us to continue the work He began while He was here on this earth. In that context Jesus does promise that *if* we are working with Him as His partner in ministry, that *if* we have a need as we carry out that ministry, we are to ask, and He will meet that need.

He is not talking about our personal wants and desires. I cannot say, "Jesus, You promised to give me whatever I ask You for, so give me a 2017 Tesla Model C car with automatic pilot." That kind of request would show that I am not partnering with Him; I am trying to use Him for my own selfish desires and ambitions. And I shouldn't be disappointed when God says no to that request.

So what does it mean when Jesus invites us to *ask*? May I suggest that when Jesus shows you a need, it is because He wants you to do something about that need. If you will step out in faith and try to meet it, God will supply the resources to make it possible. Let me illustrate this with what God is doing here at Paradise Valley.

As we began the language school, we realized we needed someplace where the students could get work experience. We *asked* God what we should do, and felt Him leading us to open a thrift store. For several years my wife and I had enjoyed going to estate sales, particularly in the nicer communities. We rarely bought anything, but we left our business card with the comment that if they needed a nonprofit charity to pick up what was left after the sale, we would be willing to help them.

We had been getting enough donations to hold two rummage sales each year to generate significant income for our ministry. This has grown through the years, and now not only do we continue to conduct two rum-mage sales a year but we also supply our thrift store with good-quality clothing, furniture, and decorative items.

Then we realized we needed to pay the refugee students who were working in our thrift store. We *asked* God to guide us. We soon discov-ered that the local community college had a work-study program that the students could take advantage of. Once they had learned enough English to attend evening classes at the college, they could get a job either at our thrift store or for another employer, and the state would rebate 75 percent of their salary to the employer. So our student workers receive California minimum wage, but we pay only a quarter of that out of our budget. This helps the students and it helps us, and further good news for them is that they don't lose any of their other government aid.

Many of the refugees have struggled tremendously with depression. This isn't surprising if you stop and think about what they have been through—civil war, ethnic cleansing, religious intolerance, the murder or disappearance of family members, and threats to their own lives. They have left behind their homeland, their heritage, their family members and friends, their favorite foods, and everything that's familiar to them. United Nations representatives told them one day to go to the airport, and the next thing they knew, they were in this new land.

The refugees had been told that America is a land of opportunity, but when they arrived they couldn't speak the language and couldn't get a job. Everything is so drastically different from anything they have ever known. Everything moves quickly. Everyone wants them to make appointments and be on time. Many of the refugees have never been to school a day in their life, and have come from agrarian societies where they grew everything they needed. They have no idea what it means to work for someone else and get paid for it. It's no wonder that they are depressed.

We *asked* God what we could ever do about their depression. God reminded us of something we had read somewhere, to the effect that getting one's hands into the soil is therapeutic to the mind and body. We felt impressed to start a community garden. We leased some property for $1.00 from the Paradise Valley Hospital, our next-door neighbor, and planted a garden. It has grown to cover well over three acres.

The refugees began to sing and chatter together as they worked outdoors and were reminded of the good things from their homeland.

As they began working the soil and planting their seeds, a miracle occurred: the depression lifted! The refugees began to sing and chatter together as they worked outdoors and were reminded of the good things

Chapter 4 Ask

from their homeland. This of course had an effect on their ability to learn English, as well. As their depression lessened they were able to study better.

We saw that many of the refugees had little concept of health and hygiene. Again we *asked*, and God led us, through one of our members, to partner with Azusa Pacific University. The school sends nursing students to our center every Tuesday. They check people's blood pressure in the morning, during our food distribution. Then they go downstairs to the fellowship hall, fix a good lunch for the students, and teach them basic health and hygiene.

We soon saw that many of the refugee families were limited and often not able to make it to class because of the need for childcare for their young children. This area was too much for us to take on, so we prayed, asking God for a solution. One of our volunteer ESL teachers said, "My brother has a nonprofit charity, and he has had a number of childcare facilities over the years. Let me check with him. To make a long story short, God opened doors, and soon we had a child development center open in our church's children's classrooms. It has become a great blessing to our church, community, and refugees. It has even become a job-training site for some of our students.

Another need we saw was a huge one—medical and dental help for both our struggling refugees and underemployed residents of our community. We *asked* God what He would have us do. The Adventist Medical Evangelism Network (AMEN) was scheduled to hold its annual convention here in San Diego that year. One of their officers called and asked us if we saw a need for a weekend medical/dental clinic. That weekend we were blessed to partner with AMEN and serve more than 300 people in our community with everything from cleaning teeth to root canals and

Catherine cooks lunches for the ESL students, often including fresh garden produce. She holds a stem of lenga-lenga, also known as amaranth. Behind her right shoulder is cassava. The tall plant over her left shoulder is sugar cane, being grown as an experiment.

crowns. What a blessing that was! You can see a video of that story on our web page: www.FriendshipsForHope.org under Featured Stories.

As we have been learning how to *ask,* there has been a group of our church members who have discovered the joys of intercessory prayer life, and a small group of prayer warriors is now growing and meeting weekly to pray for God's guidance and leadership at our church. This is but another indication that God is in control and leading our church forward to do His will.

Right now we need to find additional sources of funding for our rapidly growing ministry. We have been praying and *asking* God to teach us how to share our need with our community and ask for support.

We were drawn to talk to the president of the Alliance for African Assistance, a resettlement agency in our community that often sends us new students. As we talked with him, we learned that they began much like we did, with a garage where they had a sale each week to raise money so they could work with refugees. They have grown during the past 30 years to where they have industries and businesses that generate all the income they need for their ministry. Their story has inspired us and assured us that God will continue to provide the resources if only we are faithfully doing what He shows us to do.

The Alliance for African Assistance has agreed to partner with us and help us learn better ways to work with our refugee families and find ways to grow and become a self-reliant ministry as they have. We feel that God is leading us to start microenterprises at which we can provide employment for many refugees while also generating income for our program. We don't yet know where the money or expertise will come from for this, but we are confident that if this thought is from God, He will open the doors as He has so far.

As we are teaching the refugees to become self-sufficient, we need to model this same principle and become self-sufficient ourselves. It will take time and money to get there, but we feel compelled to move in that direction.

It is exciting to see that as we *ask*, God answers. This is exactly what Jesus is saying here in our text: "You may ask me for anything in my name, and I will do it" (John 14:14). We have *asked* and He has abundantly supplied our needs as we have partnered with Him.

Our youth group has caught the vision and is now hosting Drive-Through Prayer times, almost like a car wash, where they stand on the street with signs inviting drivers to stop and be prayed for. This is proving

Chapter 4   Ask

very popular and is also revitalizing the spirituality of our youth. They have recently begun to prepare care packages of health and hygiene items for some of the 7,000 homeless on the streets of San Diego and are going downtown on weekends to give these out.

When you decide to enter that partnership and accept Jesus' invitation to go, what do you have to offer? All we have is ourselves. We give ourselves to Jesus and respond as Isaiah did: "I heard the voice of the Lord saying, 'Whom shall I send? And who will go for us?' And I said, 'Here am I. Send me!'" (Isa. 6:8).

Although, like Isaiah, we are willing, we really have nothing but that willingness to give to this partnership to which God calls us. We are incapable of accomplishing the task; God has to take us and grow us into what He needs.

As He grows us, challenges and obstacles stretch us and help us grow. It is only as we are stretched beyond our own capabilities that we actually grow. In this context, Jesus makes the offer: "Whoever believes in me will do the works I have been doing, and they will do even greater things than these" (John 14:12).

And when we go in response to Jesus' invitation, we have this promise, "I will do whatever you ask in my name, so that the Father may be glorified in the Son. You may ask me for anything in my name, and I will do it" (verses 13, 14).

A young couple is blessed with children. God entrusts them to raise these children for Him. They find that they need an extra amount of patience in dealing with their parenting responsibilities. They pray and ask for patience. How is God going to answer that prayer? Is patience something He can just pour into them? No, God develops and grows patience within them as they face challenges together with Him.

Patience, in actuality, is the result of the partnership with God. The Bible speaks of it as part of the fruit of the Spirit. "But the fruit of the Spirit is love, joy, peace, patience, kindness, goodness, faithfulness gentleness, and self-control. There is no law against things like this" (Gal. 5:22, 23, CEB).

As they ask, and He helps them make it through each challenge victoriously, they grow. It is not going to happen overnight, but gradually as they continue to grow, and as they continue in their partnership with God, patience develops in their lives.

The student at school is mistreated and is tempted to lash back in retaliation against those who have mistreated him, but then he remembers reading in the Bible, "Do not repay evil with evil or insult with insult. On the contrary, repay evil with blessing, because to this you were called so that you may inherit a blessing" (1 Peter 3:9).

Is this going to be easy to do? Is it something the student can do by himself? No! It can happen only when he has surrendered his life to Jesus and God is living in him. He doesn't have the ability to live that kind of life on his own.

The worker in the workplace needs to learn to be faithful in all of her dealings. She will face opportunities to make right or wrong choices. As she partners with God and comes through those challenges successfully, she will grow in her faithfulness and honesty in the workplace.

As Jesus taught us when He was here, "Whoever can be trusted with very little can also be trusted with much, and whoever is dishonest with very little will also be dishonest with much. So if you have not been trustworthy in handling worldly wealth, who will trust you with true riches? And if you have not been trustworthy with someone else's property, who will give you property of your own?" (Luke 16:10–12).

None of us has all the skills and abilities to meet every challenge we face, but as we continue to grow, and to *ask* God for the things we need, He will grow us, until we are able to be faithful, kind, and trustworthy. Together with God, we will be able to accomplish great and marvelous things, even greater things than Jesus did when He was here on earth. That is Jesus' promise.

None of us has all the skills and abilities to meet every challenge we face, but as we continue to grow, and to ask *God for the things we need, He will grow us, until we are able to be faithful, kind, and trustworthy.*

Why will these things be greater? Because we are fallen, sinful, and weak. We can do nothing ourselves. But as we surrender to God, we have access to His power and abilities. This is what the partnership is all about.

Now, because we are human and sinful and make mistakes, sometimes we will blow it and cause ourselves problems. This will often make the ultimate accomplishment of God's purposes and plans for our lives more

Chapter 4   Ask

difficult. But because we are in partnership with God, He has promised that He will still be with us and go through these times together with us.

One of my favorite promises in the Bible is this one in Romans 8:26–28: "The Spirit helps us in our weakness. We do not know what we ought to pray for, but the Spirit himself intercedes for us through wordless groans. And he who searches our hearts knows the mind of the Spirit, because the Spirit intercedes for God's people in accordance with the will of God. And we know that in all things God works for the good of those who love him, who have been called according to his purpose."

Even though we are weak, and often do not even know what to *ask* for, because we are in this partnership with God, His Spirit will *ask* for the right things for us. And, in addition, God promises that through all of this He is working for our ultimate and best good. Whether we do something wrong, or circumstances beyond our control bring us setbacks, God nonetheless is still growing us to be all that He created us to be.

All too often we forget to ask for help, and facing life alone, we become overwhelmed. Asking for help is not a magic wand. But acknowledging that God is there walking with us, and that nothing catches Him by surprise, can certainly help us to face the issues we are up against.

I have found that remembering His promise that "in all things God works for the good of those who love him, who have been called according to his purpose" often helps me to face my issues successfully. Each success strengthens me for the next issue. Remember, God is not the author of sickness, suffering, evil, or other trials, but He is the God who has been through it all before us and knows how to get us where He is taking us.

It was not easy for Jesus in the Garden of Gethsemane when He pleaded with God: "'Father, if you are willing, take this cup from me; yet not my will, but yours be done.' An angel from heaven appeared to him and strengthened him. And being in anguish, he prayed more earnestly, and his sweat was like drops of blood falling to the ground" (Luke 22:42–44).

Jesus' Father didn't remove the suffering from Him, but He sent an angel to strengthen Him to go through it. He promises the same for you and me. He feels our trials. He knows what we are going through. And He will strengthen us to survive whatever we are going through so that we can be victorious and bring glory to God through the process.

Sometimes it helps to look back at some of those who have gone before us. Many of God's faithful children suffered greatly at the hands of evil people, even dying as martyrs, but God was with them and strengthened them for whatever they faced.

The author of Hebrews talks a lot about those who walked with God, and he gives us this assurance: "Since we have a great high priest who has ascended into heaven, Jesus the Son of God, let us hold firmly to the faith we profess. For we do not have a high priest who is unable to empathize with our weaknesses, but we have one who has been tempted in every way, just as we are—yet he did not sin. Let us then approach God's throne of grace with confidence, so that we may receive mercy and find grace to help us in our time of need" (Heb. 4:14–16).

It wasn't easy for Jesus, and life isn't promised to be easy for us, but because of Jesus we can live at peace in the present and face the future with confidence! He will see that we are victorious.

When the challenges of life face you each day, keep your eyes focused on Jesus, the author and the finisher of your faith. When our eyes are on our problems, they can seem insurmountable. When we turn and look to Jesus and His promises, we can face the day unafraid, filled with confidence.

Five hundred or more local families receive food and clothing from Paradise Valley Church's Community Services Center every week. The taller building in the background is Paradise Village, a retirement community from which residents can look out their windows every day and observe activities on the church's campus.

Chapter 5
Love

This is love: not that we loved God, but that he loved us
and sent his Son as an atoning sacrifice for our sins.
1 John 4:10.

What would it mean to be partners with God in the real world we live in today? We have seen that God has called us to go and share with the world what He means to us. We have seen that even though we are all broken, sinful individuals, as we go, God will grow us into the people we need to be. He tells us to ask for whatever we need to do the work He wants to do through us.

But have you grasped the full significance of what God wants to give to this partnership, and in turn what He calls us to share?

It's what our world needs more than anything else. God wants us to experience the reality of knowing that He truly loves us. It must be more than head knowledge. It comes from experiencing firsthand the love of God.

The realization also hit me that we can't share what we haven't yet experienced for ourselves. If we don't know what it means to be God's beloved son or daughter, then all we have to share are words written in an ancient book, and they will have very little impact. But the Bible is much more than just a book of teachings, more than a list of rules and regulations. It is a practical guidebook for our lives. And it contains the story of Jesus, our example.

As Jesus steps out and begins the ministry His Father has called Him to, we see Him at the Jordan River. John the Baptist has been preparing the way for Him, calling the nation of Israel to repentance and baptism. Jesus shows up one day to be baptized.

"Then Jesus came from Galilee to the Jordan to be baptized by John. But John tried to deter him, saying, 'I need to be baptized by you, and do you come to me?' Jesus replied, 'Let it be so now; it is proper for us to do this to fulfill all righteousness.' Then John consented. As soon as Jesus was baptized, he went up out of the water. At that moment heaven was opened, and he saw the Spirit of God descending like a dove and alighting on him. And a voice from heaven said, 'This is my Son, whom I love; with him I am well pleased'" (Matt. 3:13–17).

Did you know that God says He loves us, too? Look what He says to us in 1 John 4:9, 10: "This is how God showed his love among us: He sent his one and only Son into the world that we might live through him. This is love: not that we loved God, but that he loved us and sent his Son as an atoning sacrifice for our sins."

God showed us at Jesus' baptism that He loved Jesus. God showed us at Jesus' death that He loves us even more. He was willing to sacrifice His one and only, beloved Son in order to save you and me. It is not about what we have done for God; it is all about what He has done for us!

> *It is not about what we have done for God; it is all about what He has done for us!*

Many of us still don't understand this, because we haven't fully experienced it in our own life. It's not what we have done for God, but what He has done for us! Read it again: "This is love: not that we loved God, but that he loved us and sent his Son as an atoning sacrifice for our sins" (*Ibid.*). God loves you so much He was willing to give up His Son Jesus for you!

We have all grown up believing the lies the world has taught us. We believe we're not good enough. We keep trying to become good enough but never get there. Or if we don't struggle with our self-worth, we struggle with arrogance, which is really just trying to appear better than we know we really are. It all stems from a wrong picture of who we are.

Chapter 5   Love

Most of the issues of life—drug addiction, alcoholism, hoarding possessions or wealth, gambling, lying, stealing, materialism, and we could go on to name more—are all indications that we don't understand how valuable we are to God. We don't understand what it means to be a son or daughter of God.

We run around trying to find meaning, purpose, and value from all the wrong places. We cannot find true meaning and value from the gods of this earth. It is not what you are able to accumulate here and now. It is not even fame or fortune that will give you meaning and value. Some of the most miserable people in our world are the rich and famous. Don't envy them. Wealth and fame are not where it's at!

Jesus, as He begins His ministry, is baptized, and He hears God's affirmation, "This is my Son, whom I love; with him I am well pleased." From that experience the Scriptures tell us that Jesus is led out into the wilderness, where He spends the next forty days fasting and praying. As He ends those forty days of prayer, Satan comes to test and try him.

"After fasting forty days and forty nights, he was hungry. The tempter came to him and said, 'If you are the Son of God, tell these stones to become bread.' Jesus answered, 'It is written: "Man shall not live on bread alone, but on every word that comes from the mouth of God."' Then the devil took him to the holy city and had him stand on the highest point of the temple. 'If you are the Son of God,' he said, 'throw yourself down. For it is written: "He will command his angels concerning you, and they will lift you up in their hands, so that you will not strike your foot against a stone." Jesus answered him, 'It is also written: "Do not put the Lord your God to the test."' Again, the devil took him to a very high mountain and showed him all the kingdoms of the world and their splendor. 'All this I will give you,' he said, 'if you will bow down and worship me.' Jesus said to him, 'Away from me, Satan! For it is written: "Worship the Lord your God, and serve him only."' Then the devil left him, and angels came and attended him" (Matt. 4:2–11).

Sometimes we get sidetracked thinking about the various things Satan tempted Jesus with and try to say that these three temptations cover everything we are tempted with. I don't think that is the real issue here. The real issue is that Satan was trying to plant a seed of doubt in Jesus' mind. He said, "*If* you are the Son of God." If Satan could get that seed of doubt to grow in Jesus' mind, he would have been successful in overthrowing Jesus.

Do I hear you say, "Yes, Jesus is the Son of God, but I am not God's son or daughter"? That is one of Satan's most successful lies. If you have accepted Jesus as your Lord and Savior, you are a son or daughter of God.

"To all who did receive him, to those who believed in his name, he gave the right to *become* children of God—children born not of natural descent, nor of human decision or a husband's will, but born of God" (John 1:12, 13, italics supplied).

We are sons and daughters of God, and about us God says, "This is my son/daughter whom I love; with him/her I am well pleased."

The partnership God wants to have with us is the relationship of a *loving father* with his son or daughter. Many of us have had our sinful earthly fathers let us down and even hurt us, but our heavenly Father loves us with an unconditional everlasting love. He wants us to know without a doubt that we are His sons and daughters, and He loves unconditionally. Absolutely nothing we can do will cause Him to stop loving us.

When we really understand that truth, no lie from the devil will have power over us. Nor is there any temptation that, together with our Father, we cannot resist and be victorious over.

Satan says, "If you will just gamble some of God's money that He has given you to manage, I will give you a lot more." We will recognize that as a lie, a trap from Satan. We don't want to risk God's money at the casino.

When Satan says, "If you can just accumulate enough possessions, you will really be someone special," we will recognize it as a lie. What we accumulate on this earth does not make us special; it will all be burned up someday soon. Being a son or daughter of God is what makes us special.

Satan's suggestion that "if you just numb your mind with alcohol or drugs, all your problems will disappear" is just another lie.

When we recognize that we are children of a loving heavenly Father, we will recognize that thoughts of low self-worth and arrogance that flood our minds are deceptions from the evil one. Not only will we recognize the lies of the deceiver, but God will be there to lead us away from those lies.

God wants us to understand what this partnership means to Him. It is more than just our going and doing, with Him providing for our needs as we minister together with Him. He wants us to go beyond that, to experience what it means to be a beloved son or daughter of His. When we experience that we are children of God, whom He values and loves, then we will have new power in our lives to face the deceptions of the devil.

As God said to Jeremiah, "Before I formed you in the womb I knew you, before you were born I set you apart; I appointed you as a prophet to the nations" (Jer. 1:5). He says the same thing to each of us: "Before I formed you in the womb I knew you, before you were born I set you apart; I appointed you ..."

Chapter 5   Love

It's not just God's prophets who are set apart for a specific purpose. Every one of us was created for a special purpose also. He has gifted you for what He wants to accomplish through you as you work with Him. Your abilities are all His abilities. All of us are called to partner with our Father God. He has a special plan for each of us. As he told Jeremiah, "I know the plans I have for you, ... plans to prosper you and not to harm you, plans to give you hope and a future" (Jer. 29:11).

That is our Father speaking to us, His children. That God has a special plan for each of us shouldn't come as a surprise. Don't we parents have plans and aspirations for our children? Don't we want the best for each of them? God wants the best for you as His child too.

Unfortunately, just because we want the best for our children doesn't mean that they will always choose the best. God wants the best for us, but we have the freedom to choose, and many do not make the choice to follow God's full will for their lives.

We often choose to live *with* our sins. We often choose to accept the deceptions Satan throws at us. I urge you to not do that, but rather to understand God's grace and accept the love and value God places on your life.

Allow God to hold you close. Feel His loving arms around you, and hear Him tell you how very special and loved you are. May you know the value He places upon your life and respond positively to all that He wants for you.

The psalmist invites us to "taste and see how good the Lord is! The one who takes refuge in him is truly happy!" (Ps. 34:8, CEB).

What excites me almost as much as the impact we are having on the refugee community in San Diego is the impact "tasting and seeing" is having on the members of our church. We are a vibrant, active congregation with close to 125 members involved in outreach ministries to our community. This doesn't count the many others who lead out in the services at church each weekend. The love they share each week with members of the church community bubbles over to include the community. We have become the loving, caring, compassionate church that Jesus created and designed us to be.

Our Community Services volunteers come each Tuesday to share God's love in tangible real ways with the community around us. As they give food and clothing each week, they are also giving a whole lot more in the love they share through their actions and words.

God continues to bring us new members. We baptize between thirty and forty people a year. Many of these people were volunteering in our ministries long before they joined the church, so once they join the family, they continue doing what they have already been doing. In November 2015 we celebrated our fourth year of ministry to refugees with a parade of members carrying flags representing the sixty-two nationalities worshiping together at our church. For those not yet fluent in English, we translate our worship services into Arabic, French, Kinyarwanda, Laotian, Spanish, and Swahili.

As we have begun to understand how much God loves us, we feel genuine love for one another. We still have room to grow, but God is living in and through us, and we are beginning to see the results of His love flowing through us to others. People tell us they notice the difference as soon as they walk onto our campus.

Kap and Juliet relax at a Paradise Valley Church picnic. Originally from Myanmar, they spent time in India and Malaysia before being resettled in San Diego. Both of them serve the church, Kap as a deacon and Juliet as a deaconess.

Two of our newer members, Kap and Juliet, have experienced that love. Because the government of Myanmar (formerly known as Burma) would not allow them to work or to live their Christian faith, Kap and his wife, Juliet, fled as refugees to India. Juliet had been a seamstress and Kap a businessman in their home country. After sojourns in India and Malaysia, they and their two children were relocated to San Diego.

Kap and Juliet both volunteer part time, she at P. V. Thrift Store and he in our Refugee Assimilation Project. They have both learned English, and both are taking college courses. Kap is moving toward a degree in nursing, while Juliet is studying clothing design. At church Kap serves as a deacon and Juliet as a deaconess. Thanks to some generous donors, and sacrifice on their own part, both of their children are attending our nearby Christian school.

Chapter 5 Love

"After two years here, we feel comfortable, like real family," Juliet has told us. "We don't have much money, but because God and people we don't know [donors] have helped us, we are happy."

After two years here, we feel comfortable, like real family.

This story is repeated again and again as our community and refugee friends come and join our family. We are God's heart, arms, hands, and feet to love them, because He first loved us. As we have experienced God's love, we, in turn, through our partnership with God, are able to pass on that love to those God brings to us. What a privilege is ours to pass on what God has given us!

This idea of passing it on can best be illustrated by a pitcher, cup, saucer, and plate. God, represented by the pitcher, is the source of everything. As He pours His life into us, the cup, we soon overflow to the saucer, our family, and then to the plate, our community and ultimately to our world. Only as we keep receiving does anything overflow to others. The moment we forget the source of our love and stop receiving, we also stop giving.

God impacting our world through us.

*And this gospel of the kingdom will be preached in the whole world
as a testimony to all nations, and then the end will come.*
Matthew 24:14

This is why it is so vital that we understand that we are sons and daughters of God, that God loves us, and that we are special to Him. We must continue growing every day in our partnership with God so that we can pour out the love we experience to those around us.

Recent students at our language school have been Arabic-speaking refugees from Iraq, Afghanistan, Syria, and other neighboring countries. Many of them are Muslim. It is rewarding to see how God's love is soaked up by these refugees who know about God, but who have not experienced His love. They are acquainted with a God of rules and regulations, but as they become acquainted with the love of God through us, it is changing their lives.

It is exciting to have baby dedications in our church for Muslim families, and to be there to help meet their daily physical, emotional, and spiritual needs. As we welcome them into our family they are finding a whole new relationship with their God and their Elder Brother, Jesus Christ. We recently welcomed one officially into our church family. Others are studying, hungry to learn more. As they learn of God's love for His children, and as they experience that love for the first time, they find a peace and joy that they have never experienced before.

Today, as the Muslim world is feared by much of the rest of the world and religious intolerance is becoming more prevalent, God has sent us with a message of love and acceptance for *all* of His children. Hindus, Buddhists, Muslims, atheists, Catholics, Protestants, and agnostics all are loved by our God, and He calls us to share His love with them. What a different world it would be if instead of spreading fear and hatred we shared the love of God with those who so desperately need to know His love! If all they ever hear or feel from us is hatred, we will never be able to reach them with His love.

God's love is the most powerful change agent in the world! What a privilege we have to share God's love in a world so much in need of it. We live in a love-starved world today. Everything is moving so fast, and relationships are becoming difficult to find time to develop and nurture. But as we take that time, and build loving, caring relationships with those God brings us into contact with, His love makes a difference.

Have you experienced God's love lately? If so, let it flow, pass it on to others who so desperately need it.

Chapter 6
Choose

But if serving the Lord seems undesirable to you,
then choose for yourselves this day whom you will serve. . .
But as for me and my household, we will serve the Lord.
Joshua 24:15.

The world watched the United States as the Pope visited our country and spoke before Congress. This is the first time a major religious leader has spoken to the political leaders of our country.

We have seen a number of earthquakes around the Pacific Rim, with one as large as 8.3 magnitude in Chile, and people all around the Pacific are fearful of tidal waves.

We are seeing a tremendous upsurge in mass shootings—Roseburg, Oregon; San Bernardino, California; Orlando, Florida; and the list goes on. Add this to the moon looking like blood recently, and we are reminded of the words of Jesus: "There will be signs in the sun, moon and stars. On the earth, nations will be in anguish and perplexity at the roaring and tossing of the sea. People will faint from terror, apprehensive of what is coming on the world, for the heavenly bodies will be shaken. At that time they will see the Son of Man coming in a cloud with power and great glory.

When these things begin to take place, stand up and lift up your heads, because your redemption is drawing near." (Luke 21:25--28).

These things should not make us worried and afraid; rather, we should be looking up with great anticipation, knowing that God's Word is sure, and that Jesus is returning soon to take us home. This is what we have been longing for! To me all of this gives a greater reason to believe in the subject of this book, partnering with God, because this is why it is important to choose to have a close partnership with Him. We can know all about the last-day events and what to expect before Christ returns, but if we are not personally ready for that great event, it will fill our hearts with fear when we see the signs fulfilling around us.

God does not want us to be fearful. He wants us to be ready. The only way we can be ready for the second coming of Christ is to choose to have Him living in us, in this special partnership we have been exploring together.

We have seen that God has asked us to go with Him and share His love to a world in desperate need of Him. And as we begin that journey, we must surrender the idea that we are capable of doing anything in and of ourselves. We have explored Christ's invitation to ask Him for the resources we need to accomplish the task, because it is too great for us. We know that we are God's beloved children. As our heavenly Father, He won't withhold any good thing from us as He shares His love through us.

Looking at partnership further, we are going to discover together that not only do we choose to surrender ourselves to God but that He also chooses us. He says: "You are a chosen people, a royal priesthood, a holy nation, God's special possession, that you may declare the praises of him who called you out of darkness into his wonderful light. Once you were not a people, but now you are the people of God; once you had not received mercy, but now you have received mercy" (1 Peter 2:9, 10). Don't you just love that? You are chosen. You are God's special possession.

Once we recognize that God has chosen us, and we choose to accept that chosenness and partner with God, we begin to accomplish everything God needs to accomplish through us. Once we open the door to Him, God

> *You are God's special possession.*

enters and does great things in and through us! He's the One who does those things; we are just privileged to be His human helpers.

Chapter 6   Choose

This idea of being chosen by God is different from what we often understand as being chosen by others. When we chose teams when I was a child, I was often ignored. Other children didn't want me on their team because I wasn't good enough. I wasn't good at sports because my eyes had been damaged at birth, and I didn't see well. I didn't grow up with a healthy concept of being chosen.

In the broken ideas of the world, one gets chosen at someone else's expense. I didn't make the team because someone else who was better at that particular sport was chosen instead. This is not the way it is with God! God chooses us not because of our abilities, but because we're His children, and He loves us. All He asks is that we be open to His call and choose Him in return.

God's love for us makes it possible for us to love others. It is the same way with His choosing us. We are His choice not because we are better than anyone else, but just because He created and made us who we are. He chose us even before we were born.

As God said to Jeremiah, "Before I formed you in the womb I knew you, before you were born I set you apart; I appointed you as a prophet to the nations" (Jer. 1:5). This speaks of our chosenness. No, we are not all chosen to be a prophet as Jeremiah was, but God did form us and create us and choose us for a special, specific purpose.

1 Peter 2:9 calls God's chosen people "a royal priesthood" and "a holy nation." The idea of royal priesthood speaks of the spiritual part of our ministry together with God. We are to be spiritual messengers to our community, sharing God's love and grace through our words and actions.

Some people read "holy nation" as though it is speaking of the United States being a holy nation, and they try to reform the country and make it "holy." That's not what this is talking about. This is not a message to any particular nation or country, but a message to God's people, those who have chosen to live in a close, living, personal relationship with Him.

As His holy nation we are to be a living example before the world of what it means to recognize God as our source of authority and power. We have the privilege to live before our community, showing them what it means to be chosen by God to live with and for God.

There is a retirement community that wraps around two sides of our church. It sits four stories high, so there is a lot of opportunity for residents to sit at their windows and watch the activity at our church. We get comments on a regular basis about how they are watching us, and they are amazed at the daily activities they see going on.

They watch as seniors arrive on Mondays and Fridays for the senior stretch exercise class and as trucks arrive daily with food for distribution to the community. The residents next door watch each Tuesday as more than 400 people line up at our doors to receive more than 10,000 pounds of food and clothing each week. They see the bus arriving every morning with students from Africa, Asia, and the Middle East coming to learn English. They see them out working in the community garden.

The neighbors watch in amazement as we unload truckloads of donated household items picked up from estate sales. Then volunteers to sort, clean, and price them for either our rummage sales, thrift store, or to be given away. Retirement community residents often donate items themselves for our ministry. They have commented to us that they have never seen a church so busy serving the community.

While we don't think about it, all of us are being watched in the communities where we live. Our neighbors see our routines. They know when we are going to church and how busy we are helping others. At work or

On Tuesday mornings, when community residents pick up their weekly bag of food, a group of quilters take their place in the Community Services building at the sewing machines and quilting frame. Their main activity is making soft flannel baby quilts. The majority of these quilts go to families whose babies are dedicated at church. When Darlene, who oversees the quilting project, presents the quilts to the families, she reminds them that their babies are always "wrapped in God's love."

Chapter 6 Choose

at school, we are being observed, and people are listening to our conversations. In everything we do we are all living witnesses of our relationship to our God.

There was a time when God chose a nation; that is the story of the Old Testament. It didn't work. It failed. They didn't live before the world as an example of a nation ruled by God. So God has turned to us, the spiritual descendants of Israel, as His chosen people to live as a holy nation in the communities where we live.

1 Peter 2:9 goes on to say that God's chosen people are His "special possession." We are to live as God's possession, someone who is not their own but is actually owned by God. Paul tells us, "Do you not know that your bodies are temples of the Holy Spirit, who is in you, whom you have received from God? You are not your own; you were bought at a price. Therefore honor God with your bodies" (1 Cor. 6:19, 20).

Jesus has not only chosen us, He has actually purchased us from sin and slavery to Satan by dying for us on the cross. We are now His possession. Even our bodies belong to Him. We are to live with that knowledge. We belong to God; His Spirit is dwelling within us. We are to live as holy temples of God. This is even more personal than being His chosen nation. We are individually to be temple bodies for God to live and dwell in.

This is not how the world lives! They say, "This is *my* body. I can do what I want with it! I can put anything I want into it, tattoo or pierce it any way I like, and live any way I choose." Well, who do you choose to control your life? Have you chosen to surrender yourself to God's control, or are you demanding to be in control yourself?

God reminds us that we have been purchased at a great cost and are now to live as His people, remembering that we are the temple of God's Spirit, who lives in us. We cannot mistreat these special bodies Christ died to redeem. When we numb our minds with drugs and alcohol, it makes it impossible for us to remember our chosenness. We then act in ways that betray our relationship with God. It is all part of understanding and recognizing our chosenness. When we understand that we are God's, created unique and special for a specific purpose, it changes how we view life.

When we understand that we are God's, created unique and special for a specific purpose, it changes how we view life.

Knowing that we are chosen changes not only how we live, but how we view life and react to it. Instead reacting to how we are treated, we can release all of that to God, and let Him handle it.

Jesus Himself was abused and mistreated, yet He did not retaliate against his abusers. In the garden, just before His crucifixion, we see Him praying to His Father. Jesus' humanness was pressing in just as it does with us, and Jesus had to remind Himself that He was living within God's plan for His life.

We pick up the story in Matthew 26:36–39: "Jesus went with his disciples to a place called Gethsemane, and he said to them, 'Sit here while I go over there and pray.' He took Peter and the two sons of Zebedee along with him, and he began to be sorrowful and troubled. Then he said to them, 'My soul is overwhelmed with sorrow to the point of death. Stay here and keep watch with me.' Going a little farther, he fell with his face to the ground and prayed, 'My Father, if it is possible, may this cup be taken from me. Yet not as I will, but as you will.'"

There's His choice: *Not as I will, but as you will.* Jesus is setting us an example of what living in the chosenness of God is like. He accepted that His Father didn't take away the "cup" of suffering that lay ahead of him. "He returned to his disciples and found them sleeping. 'Couldn't you men keep watch with me for one hour?' he asked Peter. 'Watch and pray so that you will not fall into temptation. The spirit is willing, but the flesh is weak'" (verses 40, 41).

The disciples' lives are examples of what happens when we live in our own strength instead of God's. As Peter and the other disciples did, we fall asleep when we should be praying. We lose hope when we face challenges in our own strength and cause ourselves problems. Then the enemy of our souls comes and tempts us and tells us that God has abandoned us, that God has left us, that He isn't there.

When that happens, God hasn't left you—you have left Him. It's our choice, but if we choose to leave God and do it our own way, we shouldn't blame God for the dilemmas we get ourselves into. Satan loves to get our eyes off God and onto ourselves. He wants us to forget we are chosen, to do and say things that cause us problems. When Satan does this, recognize what the real issue is: we are choosing to live our life separated from God. We cause ourselves a whole lot of grief. But God has not left or abandoned us. He is still there.

Back in the garden, Jesus "went away a second time and prayed, 'My Father, if it is not possible for this cup to be taken away unless I drink it, may your will be done.' When he came back, he again found them sleep-

Chapter 6   Choose   61

ing, because their eyes were heavy. So he left them and went away once more and prayed the third time, saying the same thing. Then he returned to the disciples and said to them, 'Are you still sleeping and resting? Look, the hour has come, and the Son of Man is delivered into the hands of sinners. Rise! Let us go! Here comes my betrayer!'" (verses 42–46).

Please notice, God did not remove Jesus from imminent death on the cross, but He gave Him the strength to endure it. The issues in life that you face may not be easy, but they may actually be what God created and placed you here to do. Others watching how you live your life with God in spite of the problems will be inspired to a closer walk with God.

The issues in life that you face may not be easy, but they may actually be what God created and placed you here to do.

That was certainly the case with Jesus. That struggle in the garden was about His purpose for coming to earth. He came to die for your sins and mine, to purchase us back from bondage to sin and Satan. It was not easy for Him, but God gave Him the strength to do what He had prepared Him for.

Some of the refugees with whom we've become friends have learned this lesson better than we have, because being relocated to a country where you don't know anyone, can't talk to anyone because they don't speak your language, and therefore can't find employment takes an enormous amount of strength and determination.

One of these refugees who has felt God's chosenness and learned to lean on Him for strength is Charlin. As a Christian, he couldn't in good conscience join a rebel army that was forcing young men, at the threat of death, to join its revolt against the government of Chad. To keep from being forced to join the rebels, Charlin, with his wife, Eugenie, and their two children, fled from that Central African country and came as refugees to America. Their new home was a small one-bedroom apartment near the Paradise Valley Church.

Charlin and Eugenie joined the Refugee Assimilation Project's first ESL class. Charlin was one of our first two students to begin the work-study program at P. V. Thrift Store. He and the other student, Krishna, began with small tasks such as dusting, vacuuming the carpet, and steam pressing donated clothing. They worked half days and went to school in

Charlin, right, and his wife, Eugenie, in blue, became United States citizens in February 2016. They and their three children posed with Peggy and Will James after the naturalization ceremony, proudly displaying their citizenship certificates. Originally from Chad, Charlin and Eugenie are now fluent in English and have full-time jobs. He works at Paradise Valley Hospital, and she, at Paradise Village retirement community.

the evenings. They left their six-month stints at the store having demonstrated good work ethics, been given more challenging responsibilities, and earned enough money to open and learn to manage bank accounts.

Charlin and Eugenie found love and acceptance at our church and soon joined and became active members, allowing God to work through them to touch others in the community. God has abundantly blessed and used them in their new homeland. Charlin has a full-time maintenance job at Paradise Valley Hospital, and Eugenie is a loving caregiver in the assisted living facility at the nearby Paradise Village. They were blessed with the birth of a third child after coming to San Diego. And after living for several years with their three children in a one-bedroom apartment, they have moved into a larger one.

Life is often harsh, but when we know that God is living in us and that He will never leave or forsake us, we can move forward together with

Chapter 6   Choose   63

God, as Charlin and Eugenie did. Who knows but what you have been
placed here at this time to face the trials and troubles before you, and
come out victorious on the other side, as an example that will strengthen
and help another struggling person.

God strengthened His Son Jesus to go through the trial successfully,
and He will do the same for you and me. The road ahead may not be easy,
but God has chosen you, He has created you, He has ordained you to do
something only you can do for Him. Be faithful to Him, keep your eyes
focused on Him, and join Jesus in His prayer, "My Father, if it is not possible for this cup to be taken away unless I drink it, may your will be done."

We are living in the days that Christ spoke of when He would return
and take us to our home in heaven that He has gone to prepare for us.
While we don't know exactly what will happen before He comes, He has
told us that there will be some tough days ahead. But we don't need to
face those days with fear, because we know that Jesus has promised to go
through those days together with us. If He is with us, there is nothing we
can't make it through together. I encourage you to make the choice to stay
connected to Jesus. He has chosen you, you are special to Him, and He
will be with you wherever He leads you.

Chapter 7
Bless

I will bless you; I will make your name great,
and you will be a blessing.
Genesis 12:2.

I love the song "God Bless America." It is truly God's blessing that we need as we face the uncertain future of our country together. We not only need God's blessing for our country, we need God's blessing on our individual lives. But why should God bless us? Or maybe I should be asking, "What should we be doing *when* God blesses us?"

The United States became a blessed nation because it was settled by people fleeing from other countries coming to the American continent so they could worship God according to their own conscience. The United States was established as a land of freedom: freedom to worship or not worship; freedom to believe in God, or not to believe in God; freedom to worship however you wished, or not to worship at all.

Our Constitution actually forbids our government from showing preference to any one religion over another. Some people have mistakenly gotten the idea that the United States is a Christian nation. *No*, the United States is a land of religious freedom. We are all free to worship as our own conscience guides us. This doesn't mean that we cannot as a

Chapter 7 Bless

nation receive God's blessing. God is willing to bless not only America; He is willing to bless any nation or individual who in turn will pass that blessing on to others.

This religious freedom is something that makes America unique. In many other countries of our world, the leaders mandate what your religion must be. In the United States of America, Buddhist, Catholic, Jewish, Muslim, Protestant, Mormon, Jehovah's Witness, atheist and Hindu all live together in freedom. No one has the right to force you to worship or not to worship. We are beginning to hear some discontent with that, however, and that makes me fearful, as it could mean that we would choose to walk away from God's blessing and become no different than many other countries. Freedom of choice is important to God! Jesus died to guarantee our freedom to choose.

Myanmar is one of the many countries where religion is mandated by the state. There have been many years of fighting and civil war in that country. Because of this, seven-year-old Mu and her family fled from their home in Mon State, in southern Myanmar. They spent seven years in a refugee camp in Thailand before being relocated to the multiethnic City Heights area of San Diego.

Mu's father, who had been a school headmaster in Burma and taught English in the refugee camp, attended our Refugee Assimilation Project ESL classes. Riding each morning and evening to and from school on the church's RAP bus, he became acquainted with refugee children who were attending San Diego Academy. He told Mu it was a good school, and the children were learning a lot. Mu, eager for a good-quality education, decided she wanted to attend. Generous donors to our ministry made that possible.

"Scared and nervous" when she arrived on campus, she soon made

Mu, whose father attended English classes at Paradise Valley Church, dreams of becoming a dentist. After being sponsored to attend San Diego Academy for two years, Mu graduated with honors. She is pursuing her dream by studying at a local college, learning more technical English vocabulary and taking prerequisite courses for the dental program.

friends and studied hard to earn good grades. She has graduated from high school and is attending college, hoping eventually to achieve her dream of becoming a dentist. Although she and her family are not Christians, Mu frequently attends the Paradise Valley Church with her school friends.

Another refugee mother with her three daughters also came from Myanmar two years ago. A sponsor helped one of the girls, Miriam, to attend San Diego Academy. Her English improved quickly, and she is doing well with her studies. Miriam impressed us all recently as a student presenter for the University of California at San Diego's First Annual Map Research Symposium.

Last fall Miriam applied for, and won, a coveted position in UCSD's new Mentor Assistance Program. Throughout her high school junior year she spent her spare time conducting research on the effects of stress on various strains of living cells using the university's laboratory facilities.

For many, the symposium became special when Miriam and her fellow researchers each stood by their display boards and answered questions of an inquisitive crowd. But the highlight of the afternoon was when Miriam got to stand before an audience of friends and strangers and share her research results in the form of a PowerPoint presentation. She did a beautiful job while hiding all signs of the nerves she certainly was feeling. All this from a refugee who had only a limited English vocabulary two years ago.

What a privilege is ours to be part of blessing the lives of these young people who have left all they have ever known and come to a strange country, where God has given us the opportunity to help them find their place in life.

One of our refugee fathers who is struggling, is in poor health and unable to find employment, recently handed me an envelope with $25 in it to help with our ministry. He realized our need as I had sent out a letter to all of our members asking for support, and he responded with a sacrificial gift to bless us back. He has been blessed by us and in turn wants to pass on that blessing. His story is illustrated by the story of Abraham, which is recorded in the very first book of the Bible.

God came to Abraham one day and said to him, "Go from your country, your people and your father's household to the land I will show you. I will make you into a great nation, and I will bless you; I will make your name great, and you will be a blessing" (Gen. 12:1, 2).

Here we see God telling Abraham that He would bless him and make him great, but the reason for that blessing was so Abraham would *be* a blessing. He blesses us today for the very same reason. He wants us to bless others. Throughout the Old Testament we find the fathers pronouncing God's blessing upon their children, passing on the blessing God gave to Abraham.

We are beginning to experience what God told to Abraham so long ago: "I will bless you; … and you will be a blessing" (verse 2). When God blesses us, He gives us the opportunity to become a blessing to others.

Many of our members and volunteers are discovering the joy of doing this. Jeanne is a young woman who is a former fire fighter. She is a new convert to Christ, and as she has received His blessing, she has been coming to our Community Services center five to six days a week, tirelessly giving of her time and energy to bless others.

Jeanne and her little blue pickup truck frequently can be seen almost every day at Community Services, particularly at rummage sale time. Here, she rests momentarily beside an enormous box of carrots she has just helped unload from the Feeding America truck.

Jeanne goes out with her little blue pickup truck nearly every day, collecting food from stores or going on estate sale pickups to get donated items for our ministry. Jeanne says, "When someone says 'God bless you,' I immediately turn it around in my mind and pray that God will bless another person." She says, "When you are doing God's work you are blessed and in turn need to bless someone else."

When you are doing God's work you are blessed and in turn need to bless someone else.

Vern, an 80-year-old retired optician, volunteers daily with his pickup truck gathering donated items from stores and keeping our pantry stocked and organized for distribution. Tuesday mornings, when we distribute

Every Tuesday morning, Vern, Community Services' recycler-in-chief, tears down and disposes of empty boxes that once contained food from Feeding America or the Food Bank of San Diego.

food to community residents, he stands outside the Community Services center breaking down cardboard produce cartons for recycling. He says, "I think this is a great ministry, and I want to keep volunteering as long as God gives me health. It gives me great joy to be helping others in need."

Dorothy, even though she has celebrated her 101st birthday and is headed for 102, is at our center two days a week sorting, cleaning, and pricing items for our thrift store and rummage sales. She finds great fulfillment giving of her time to bless our ministry and help others.

"This ministry is a great part of my life," says Dorothy. "I have been in the church since 1983, and I will volunteer until the Lord comes."

Marcy, a retired schoolteacher who taught English at San Diego Academy, spends two hours each morning, Monday through Friday, teaching English as a second language to our refugee family. She says: "As Christians we are commissioned to serve God. He calls us to serve in many ways; it can be our time or expertise or our financial assistance to someone in need. I don't do it for what I can get back; I never expect someone to pay me back when I have been nudged by God to serve. The payment I receive from those I help comes in their thank-you hugs, tears, and smiles. I often forget what I have done for others, but they seem to be touched forever."

As with a number on our team, even before Theresa became a member of our church she was volunteering at our center. She says: "I have never known of a church doing so much for the community. This church

Chapter 7   Bless

reaches out in so many ways to our community, to the refugees and to the poor. I believe that because we are doing so much, God is blessing us more and more, and we in turn are able to increase our blessing to others. I came as a baby Christian, and am growing daily in my walk with God. This church is helping me to be more open and accepting of others."

We are discovering the truth of the proverb that says, "The generous will themselves be blessed, for they share their food with the poor" (Prov. 22:9). Also this one: "A faithful person will be richly blessed, but one eager to get rich will not go unpunished" (Prov. 28:20).

As we share God's blessings, we discover that in reality we receive many more blessings in return. The goal of the Christian is not to get rich and gain advantages for yourself, but to give of what God has blessed you with. As we faithfully do that, we find God continues to pour out his blessings to us.

One day when Jesus was feasting in the home of one of the Pharisees He said, "When you give a luncheon or dinner, do not invite your friends, your brothers or sisters, your relatives, or your rich neighbors; if you do, they may invite you back and so you will be repaid. But when you give a banquet, invite the poor, the crippled, the lame, the blind, and you will be blessed. Although they cannot repay you, you will be repaid at the resurrection of the righteous" (Luke 14:12–14). Jesus is telling us that if we really want to be blessed, we should give to those who have no way of paying us back.

Paul speaks of God's greatest blessing to us: "God demonstrates his own love for us in this: While we were still sinners, Christ died for us. Since we have now been justified by his blood, how much more shall we be saved from God's wrath through him! For if, while we were God's enemies, we were reconciled to him through the death of his Son, how much more, having been reconciled, shall we be saved through his life! Not only is this so, but we also boast in God through our Lord Jesus Christ, through whom we have now received reconciliation." (Rom. 5:8–11).

Jesus takes the initiative and comes to help us. While we were still sinners, before we could do anything on our own to change, He came and died for us. He paid the penalty for our sins. He came to heal the broken relationship and offers us forgiveness, so that we can once again experience a close relationship with Him. Jesus is doing what He asks us to do: bless those who have no way to pay you back. We cannot begin to pay Jesus back for what He did for us on the cross. All we can do is be grateful for what He has done and share that gift with others.

This is what He asks us to continue to do, pass along His blessing of forgiveness and reconciliation to the world around us. Just as God doesn't ask us to change ourselves before He offers us forgiveness and reconciliation with Him, we are not to ask others to change before we offer them our love and support. The reality is that we are powerless to change until we are in a close relationship with God. It is God who brings about that change in us.

Jesus instructs us: "Love your enemies, do good to those who hate you, bless those who curse you, pray for those who mistreat you. If someone slaps you on one cheek, turn to them the other also. If someone takes your coat, do not withhold your shirt from them. Give to everyone who asks you, and if anyone takes what belongs to you, do not demand it back. Do to others as you would have them do to you" (Luke 6:27–31).

What Jesus calls us to do here is exactly the opposite of our human nature. We naturally retaliate when we have been mistreated, but Jesus modeled for us what the Christian's life is to look like by uttering these words when He was hanging unjustly on the cross: "Father, forgive them, for they do not know what they are doing" (Luke 23:34).

How long has it been since you prayed that prayer about someone who unfairly hurt you? How long has it been since instead of retaliating or lashing back you simply said, "I forgive you"?

Today we are living in a world full of fear, and we are hearing that fear expressed in the church, in the school, and in politics. The apostle Paul tells us what the Christian's reaction to this should be: "Bless those who persecute you; bless and do not curse. Rejoice with those who rejoice; mourn with those who mourn. Live in harmony with one another. Do not be proud, but be willing to associate with people of low position. Do not be conceited." "If your enemy is hungry, feed him; if he is thirsty, give him something to drink. In doing this, you will heap burning coals on his head" (Rom. 12:14–16, 20).

We are discovering that many of our supposed enemies are, in fact, fearful of what we may do to them. They have been taught that *we* are the enemy, and when we follow the admonition of God, "If your enemy is hungry, feed him; if he is thirsty, give him something to drink," they react in surprise and relief and often want to know more about the God we serve.

We are honored to have a number of Muslims coming to our English language school. They come with apprehension, not knowing what to expect. As they are welcomed, respected, and treated as equals they begin to open up and share their story.

Islam can be traced directly back to the father of the Muslim religion, Abraham. Ishmael, when he left his father's house, was 14 years old, and

Abraham had taught him all that he knew about the true God. Muslims have remained faithful to the worship of the God of Abraham and Ishmael.

It is true that they do not understand about Jesus, because Jesus was not known to Abraham, except as someone to look forward too. The Muslims come to us with a curiosity about who this Jesus is. They come with many misconceptions about Christians, but as we love and accept them and pass God's blessing on to them they open up.

The Muslims come to us with a curiosity about who this Jesus is.

Muslims know nothing about God's forgiveness made possible through the death of Jesus Christ. Their religion is a religion of works and of trying hard to please God. When they learn that God loves them and forgives their sins because of Jesus, they often want to know more. What a privilege is ours to share the blessing of God with them, and tell them of the wonderful forgiveness made possible through the gift of Jesus Christ to us!

Just as Jesus took the children in His arms and blessed them when He was on this earth, we have had the privilege of dedicating children of Muslim families to God in our worship services as we pass on the blessing of God to them.

We had the happy privilege of baptizing one of our Muslim students recently. She had fled her homeland in fear for her life and had come to us for help. As she learned about God's love and blessing she asked to study the Bible with us. Today she is sharing her love for Jesus with her family back home. She shared with us that a tremendous burden rolled off of her shoulders at her baptism as she accepted and experienced the forgiveness of her sins. She is so happy that she cannot keep silent. What a blessing that she now lives in the United States, where she can experience the freedom to worship as her conscience leads her.

We ask for your prayers as we continue to minister to our Muslim, Hindu, Buddhist, and Christian refugee students, as we pass on the blessings from God here at Paradise Valley. We are praying for you as you read this book, that you will begin to understand what God wants to do through you with the blessings He has given to you.

Chapter 8
Give

Give, and it will be given to you.
A good measure, pressed down, shaken together
and running over, will be poured into your lap.
For with the measure you use, it will be measured to you.
Luke 6:38.

It's not easy being a large, multicultural church. With members from so many backgrounds, languages, cultures, and ways of looking at things, it can be difficult for us to understand one another. But the one thing we have that unites us is much stronger than the things that divide. We have God and His Holy Spirit, which unites us in God's love.

As we grow in our love for God, in turn we grow in our love and acceptance of one another. Recognizing that we are all uniquely created by our God gives us the opportunity to accept and love one another.

Of each one of us God's Word says, "Before I formed you in the womb I knew you, before you were born I set you apart; I appointed you" (Jer. 1:5).

We may share similarities, but we are not the same. Each one of us was created by God, and He has a plan for each of our lives. It is by God's

Chapter 8   Give

design that we have come together as one family here at Paradise Valley. He has given to us a unique opportunity to witness and give of ourselves to our community.

It is as God says, "You are my witnesses, … and my servant whom I have chosen, so that you may know and believe me and understand that I am he. Before me no god was formed, nor will there be one after me" (Isa. 43:10).

There is only one God, and He has chosen us to tell our community about His love. We are to model to our community what it means to be the family of God, to look to Him for our leadership, and to witness to everyone we meet about Him.

One refugee who found a church family at Paradise Valley and shares it with others is Vanessa. She was born in the Democratic Republic of Congo. Her father, a businessman, was shot and killed in the family's home by a member of one of two rebel armies from Rwanda. The rest of the family was in another part of the house, but Vanessa was in the same room with her father and witnessed his murder. She escaped and ran to another city, where she stayed for about a year, but twice she met her father's killers on the street, and they threatened to come back and kill her.

Vanessa fled to Burundi and eventually to Uganda, where she connected with a friend named Bonome, who helped her get into a refugee camp. She stayed there a month. Then she went to Kampala, where she and Bonome were married. They lived in Kampala for four years and had two children.

In late September 2011, Vanessa and her family arrived in San Diego. The Alliance for African Assistance resettlement agency moved them into an apartment on Delta Street, just a few blocks from Paradise Valley Church.

Soon after the family's arrival Vanessa met Ephraim Bendantunguka walking around her apartment complex recruiting students for our Refugee Assimilation Project's English language school, which was scheduled to open in two weeks. She joined the first class of students.

After a year at school, Vanessa began a work-study program at Paradise Village retirement community, where she was a housekeeper for three months until the birth of her second son in 2012.

In early 2014, Vanessa began working as a bagger at a local Vallarta supermarket in National City. Bonome is a case manager for ResCare, a human services organization.

Vanessa says Paradise Valley Church is "like a family to me." She lists several things the church has given her:

1. Friendship. She made friends with other students while studying English and stays in touch with them, although they have jobs in other places around the city. She remains friends with Ephraim and his wife, Regine, with one of her former English teachers, and with my wife, Peggy, and me.

2. English language skills. Vanessa had studied English in the Congo and Uganda, but she tells us that the RAP classes and Rosetta Stone computer software helped her increase her language skills "a lot."

3. Employment. I was able to help Vanessa get both her work-study experience at Paradise Village and her current job at the supermarket.

4. Food, clothing, and household necessities. "Paradise Valley helped me start my new life in America," she says. When she was expecting a baby, RAP students had a shower for her. "I never bought diapers for a year and six months, because the church provided them," she said.

5. A church family. Every year Vanessa and her family have received Christmas gifts from the church. "That means we are *very much* family," she says. She is taking Bible studies from my wife ("Peggy is a good mother for me," she says) and plans to become a Seventh-day Adventist with the encouragement of her husband.

Vanessa's biological family remains in the Congo—her mother, brothers, and sisters—and in Uganda, where a brother and his family live in a refugee camp. She keeps in touch by e-mail and Facebook but hopes that someday soon her mother, whom she hasn't seen in more than 10 years, can visit San Diego.

> *Paradise Valley helped me start my new life in America.*

What a privilege is ours to serve people like Vanessa. Most of the world operates out of selfishness, fear, and hatred, but God calls us to be different. Jesus, in His sermon on the mountain, says, "You have heard that it was said, 'Love your neighbor and hate your enemy'" (Matthew 4:43).

Isn't that the language we are hearing all around us today? "Carpet bomb them." "Destroy them all!" "Kill them before they kill us."

Jesus continues: "But I tell you, love your enemies and pray for those who persecute you, that you may be children of your Father in heaven. He causes his sun to rise on the evil and the good, and sends rain on the righteous and the unrighteous. If you love those who love you, what reward will you get? Are not even the tax collectors doing that? And if you greet only your own people, what are you doing more than others? Do not even pagans do that? Be perfect, therefore, as your heavenly Father is perfect" (verses 44–48).

Chapter 8   Give

God calls us to live differently from the world around us. He calls us to be perfect, as our heavenly Father is perfect.

How is that possible? Is Jesus asking us to do something impossible? Is He trying to frustrate us? No!

This is how the apostle Paul explained it to the Christian church in Rome: "I urge you, brothers and sisters, in view of God's mercy, to offer your bodies as a living sacrifice, holy and pleasing to God—this is your true and proper worship. Do not conform to the pattern of this world, but be transformed by the renewing of your mind. Then you will be able to test and approve what God's will is—his good, pleasing and perfect will" (Rom. 12:1, 2).

Here Paul tells us that we are to actually offer or give our lives back to God. We are to become living sacrifices, living for God and not ourselves.

He says, "Do not conform to the pattern of this world" Don't live like they do. You know what I'm talking about. You've heard people in high positions, and maybe even some of your friends, oppose bringing refugees from war-torn Middle Eastern countries into the United States because their customs and ways of worshiping God are different from ours. And if you're a student of history, you've read about how we Americans had the same attitudes in the past toward the Irish, the Italians, the Chinese, the Japanese—people we feared because they spoke different languages and behaved and worshiped differently than we did.

But God says, "Don't live like that!" Instead He tells us, "Be transformed by the renewing of your mind." It has to do with our mind, how we think. But what does that mean? How are we supposed to think?

Paul explains this further to the Christians at Philippi: "In your relationships with one another, have the same mindset as Christ Jesus: Who, being in very nature God, did not consider equality with God something to be used to his own advantage; rather, he made himself nothing by taking the very nature of a servant, being made in human likeness. And being found in appearance as a man, he humbled himself by becoming obedient to death—even death on a cross!" (Phil. 2:5–8).

If we could all have that same mind-set, would it make any difference? Would we be talking about killing others, just because they are different from us?

Back in Romans 12, Paul talks more about what this mind-set looks like in our church today: "By the grace given me I say to every one of you: Do not think of yourself more highly than you ought, but rather think of yourself with sober judgment, in accordance with the faith God has distributed to each of you. For just as each of us has one body with many members, and these members do not all have the same function, so in Christ we, though many, form one body, and each member belongs to all the others. We have different gifts, according to the grace given to each of us. If your gift is prophesying, then prophesy in accordance with your faith; if it is serving, then serve; if it is teaching, then teach; if it is to encourage, then *give* encouragement; if it is giving, then give generously; if it is to lead, do it diligently; if it is to show mercy, do it cheerfully" (verses 3–8).

Paul is telling us that just as our physical body has many parts, each one doing what it was created for, each of us has been given a gift from God to use to serve others. As each part of the body of Christ functions effectively, it will accomplish God's will.

Reading on: "Love must be sincere. Hate what is evil; cling to what is good. Be devoted to one another in love. Honor one another above yourselves. Never be lacking in zeal, but keep your spiritual fervor, serving the Lord. Be joyful in hope, patient in affliction, faithful in prayer. Share with the Lord's people who are in need. Practice hospitality" (verses 9–13).

So far you are OK with all this, right? But now here comes the hard part. Here is where God's counsel becomes difficult. God tells us what He expects us to give to others. "Bless those who persecute you; bless and do not curse. Rejoice with those who rejoice; mourn with those who mourn. Live in harmony with one another. Do not be proud, but be willing to associate with people of low position. Do not be conceited. Do not repay anyone evil for evil. Be careful to do what is right in the eyes of everyone. If it is possible, as far as it depends on you, live at peace with everyone. Do not take revenge, my dear friends, but leave room for God's wrath, for it is written: 'It is mine to avenge; I will repay,' says the Lord. On the contrary: 'If your enemy is hungry, feed him; if he is thirsty, give him something to drink. In doing this, you will heap burning coals on his head.' Do not be overcome by evil, but overcome evil with good" (verses 14–21).

Are you still OK? This is a little harder to take. It is against our human nature to feed a hungry enemy or give him a drink. That is precisely why we need to have the mind-set of Christ, which comes only by being closely connected to Him.

Are we going to overcome evil by meeting it with more evil? No! Evil will only increase the evil. Hate increases hate. Anger stirs up anger. But love overcomes evil.

Yes, I know, if you respond with love, you will be misunderstood and said to be soft and weak. But are you more worried about what people will say about you or about being an exemplary Christian and forwarding Christ's kingdom?

Chapter 8   Give

What would this world look like if Christians really did what Christ says we must do? It scares me, my friends, how many professed Christians don't appear to be living the Christian life.

What would this world look like if Christians really did what Christ says we must do?

God asks us to do something that we are physically incapable of doing. We are to give away everything He gives us. As we receive, we in turn are to give. As we talked about earlier in this book, our life is to be represented by the cup. As God, who represents the pitcher and is the source of everything, pours it into us, we must overflow and pass it on, or we will not have room to receive any more from Him. If you have it, it is because God has given it to you, and He expects you to pass it on.

Don't worry about there not being enough left for you. The God who has supplied all your needs will continue to do that. Your privilege is to pass it on.

Many have discovered the lesson of the Sea of Galilee and the Dead Sea. The Sea of Galilee receives water, but the water flows on and it is a living and vibrant lake. The Dead Sea receives its water from the Sea of Galilee, via the Jordan River, but it doesn't pass it on, and it has become a stagnant lake in which nothing can live. If we don't forward the blessing from God, we will become stagnant too. We are called to impart to others the blessings God so freely gives to each one of us. As we share what God has so generously given to us, we in turn are blessed and our life is enriched.

The apostle Paul assures us, "My God will meet all your needs according to the riches of his glory in Christ Jesus" (Phil. 4:19).

But how does this work? Jesus tells us exactly how it's done in John 15. This is my favorite chapter of the Bible. We started with the last words of Christ as recorded in Matthew. John records Christ's last message to His followers as they are walking with Jesus from the Upper Room to the Garden of Gethsemane. He is summing up everything He has been trying to teach to them for the past three-and-a-half years.

Jesus says, "I am the vine; you are the branches. If you remain in me and I in you, you will bear much fruit; apart from me you can do nothing" (John 15:5).

Without Him, we are powerless; we are broken; we, like Moses, cannot do what God asks of us. But if we stay connected to Him, nothing is impossible.

Jesus says, "If you remain in me and my words remain in you, ask whatever you wish, and it will be done for you" (verse 7). This is truly the secret to the Christian's life. Without Christ we are completely powerless, we will flounder and struggle through life. But if we will remain in that close, intimate relationship with Christ, there is no limit to what God will accomplish through us! We will look at this in more detail in the next chapter.

> *Without Him, we are powerless; we are broken.*

Why does Christ want to abide in us? Jesus tells us, "This is to my Father's glory, that you bear much fruit, showing yourselves to be my disciples" (verse 8).

God receives glory when we abide in Christ and bear fruit in our lives. This is the ultimate purpose of the Christian's life. How much glory are you giving to God through your life? Are you allowing God to live His life through you? Are you daily receiving from God so that you can give away to others what He has given you?

Remember, the more He *gives* you, the more you need to *give* away, and the more you *give* away, the more room you will have to *receive* from God. *It is impossible to out give God!*

When God shows us a need, it is because He expects us to meet that need. And when we step out in faith, He has promised to supply us with all the resources we need to meet the need.

Many of the refugee families we serve have suffered severely at the hands of people, many of whom profess to do what they do in the name of God. It is our responsibility to demonstrate to these families, who come to us from various cultural and religious backgrounds, what God is really like, and what true Christians are like.

Abbas and his Sunni family lived peacefully in a Shiite area of Baghdad until the Iraq War began in 2003. After hostile militia killed a

Abbas, originally from Baghdad, realized that fluency in English was the key to finding a good job. After taking an advanced English class at Paradise Valley Church, he found work at the airport and began studying to obtain a college degree.

Chapter 8   Give

close relative, Abbas and his wife, Zinah, fled with their children to a safer section of Baghdad and then to Turkey. In December 2011 the United Nations flew them to San Diego.

Abbas and Zinah learned about Paradise Valley Church's food distribution and English classes from neighbors. "I knew that I could get a good job if I knew English," Abbas said, so he attended the Refugee Assimilation Project's advanced English classes. Now he is studying toward a college degree that will enable him to do what he loves—work with his hands. Meanwhile, besides studying, he works full time driving cars for the Alamo car rental agency at the San Diego airport. He is providing for his family and has become productive and fruitful in his own life.

As we have given a foundation to the refugees in our community, they have built on it and are becoming able to support their families and in turn begin to pay taxes and give back to the community that supported them as they got started.

When Christ sent out the disciples, He told them, "As you go, proclaim this message: 'The kingdom of heaven has come near.' Heal the sick, raise the dead, cleanse those who have leprosy, drive out demons. Freely you have received; freely give" (Matthew 10:7, 8). The same instructions are given to us—as we have received from God, we are to give.

Chapter 9
Live

Blessed are those you choose and bring near to live in your courts!
We are filled with the good things of your house, of your holy temple.
Psalm 65:4.

How will you live your life if you are truly, completely partnering with God? I'm compelled to ask this question because I see so many professed Christians living lives that seem incompatible with how a Christian should live. I hear hateful and selfish things coming from the mouths of professed Christians. I see a lot of hate-filled Facebook posts, and I have to ask myself, is this true Christianity?

Back in the 1970s, there were a lot of people who called themselves "Jesus freaks." They asked the question WWJD? (What would Jesus do?). I've been reminded of them frequently as I've heard Christians spouting off. And I've had to ask myself, "What *would* Jesus do?"

If we are really partnering with Jesus,
and He is really living His life through us,
then we should be doing what He would do.

Chapter 9   Live   81

I think that question is relevant today, because, *if* we are really partnering with Jesus, and He is really living His life through us, then we should be doing what He would do. Isn't that true?

You see the president of the United States or any other public figure saying or doing things that you don't agree with. What would Jesus do? Would He ridicule and condemn the person on Facebook? Or would He pray for him?

You may remember the story in John 8 about a woman who was caught in the act of committing adultery being brought to Jesus. There was no question as to her sinfulness; she had been caught in the act of sin. Her accusers asked Jesus what He thought they should do with her. He didn't say a word but began to write in the dust of the ground.

When they continued to press him, what did He say? "'Let any one of you who is without sin be the first to throw a stone at her.' Again he stooped down and wrote on the ground" (John 8:7, 8).

After all her accusers had left in shame, and He was standing there alone with the sinful woman, do you remember what He said? "Jesus straightened up and asked her, 'Woman, where are they? Has no one condemned you?' 'No one, sir,' she said. 'Then neither do I condemn you,' Jesus declared. 'Go now and leave your life of sin'" (verses 10, 11).

If Jesus is living His life through us, are we going to be part of the self-righteous hypocrites who are condemning, or are we going to be like Jesus, not condemning but loving? Isn't it time we prayed for those we don't agree with us instead of condemning, judging, and criticizing?

I see and hear a lot of fear today about Muslim refugees coming into our country. It seems that many in the media have done a great job of convincing us that all Muslims are radical terrorists. They are not all terrorists. No more than all Christians are right-wing radicals who bomb abortion clinics and use violence against others who don't agree with them.

What should you do if a Muslim refugee family moves in next door to you?

Jesus told a story one time, a true story that happened just the way He told it. "On one occasion an expert in the law stood up to test Jesus. 'Teacher,' he asked, 'what must I do to inherit eternal life?' 'What is written in the Law?' he replied. 'How do you read it?'

"He answered, 'Love the Lord your God with all your heart and with all your soul and with all your strength and with all your mind'; and, 'Love your neighbor as yourself.' 'You have answered correctly,' Jesus replied. 'Do this and you will live.'

"But he wanted to justify himself, so he asked Jesus, 'And who is my neighbor?'" (Luke 10:25–29).

Here is the question for us today: Who is our neighbor? Who is it that we need to love as ourselves? Might it include Muslim refugees? It is in this setting that Jesus tells this now-famous story:

"A man was going down from Jerusalem to Jericho, when he was attacked by robbers. They stripped him of his clothes, beat him and went away, leaving him half dead. A priest happened to be going down the same road, and when he saw the man, he passed by on the other side. So too, a Levite, when he came to the place and saw him, passed by on the other side. But a Samaritan, as he traveled, came where the man was; and when he saw him, he took pity on him. He went to him and bandaged his wounds, pouring on oil and wine. Then he put the man on his own donkey, brought him to an inn and took care of him. The next day he took out two denarii and gave them to the innkeeper. 'Look after him,' he said, 'and when I return, I will reimburse you for any extra expense you may have.'

"'Which of these three do you think was a neighbor to the man who fell into the hands of robbers?' The expert in the law replied, 'The one who had mercy on him.' Jesus told him, 'Go and do likewise'" (verses 30–37).

Now, to really understand the significance of this story, you need to realize that Samaritans and Jews were enemies. They would not even talk to each other. Yet it was a Samaritan who took care of the Jew who was lying in the ditch half dead.

What are we to do if a Muslim refugee moves next door? We are to take them food, clothing, and laundry soap. We are to love them and be a friend to them, because this is probably what they are going to need, our love and friendship.

Let me share with you briefly some of the stories we are hearing daily. Abdul arrived in our area about a year ago as an asylum seeker. But for various reasons the asylum case he filed was not progressing. He asked us if we could help him by contacting immigration authorities. We sent a letter of inquiry to the local immigration office recommending him as a law-abiding person and as an educator. He was delighted when his asylum application was approved one month after we sent the letter. He commented that without the help of the church his application would have been delayed for several more months.

Abu came to us after hearing of the services we provide to refugees. He'd had to leave Iraq because his life had been threatened. He had served at a United Nations monitoring office in Baghdad. The family received clothing and food assistance for the first 12 months they were here. Abu enrolled in our ESL program and progressed in learning the language so that after eight months he was able to get a job to support his family. He continues to study English at our school because he wants to study at the local college. Abu refers all newly arriving refugee families to our school because he believes that the school provides a safe and friendly learning environment.

A mother of four children escaped their homeland after the father was killed by a religious group. She sold all they had and paid someone to smuggle them out of Afghanistan to Iran. Their short stay in Iran paved the way to continue their march to Turkey. It was January, and the snow-covered mountains of Turkey were an imposing challenge. Imagine a mother with four teenaged and young adult children (one with a young baby) marching to freedom in the middle of freezing winter. The family reached their destination in Turkey, and after four years they were accepted as refugees by the United States.

The family arrived here not knowing anyone or having any relatives here. Nor did they speak the language. One of the daughters enrolled in our English school and began her journey to a new life. The family had to depend on the church for help in every area, from food to clothing to furniture, as well as help with education at a local college. Today the three sisters and one brother are studying to earn professional degrees. The mother opens her home and welcomes us any time we visit.

Peter Thomas, left, is Paradise Valley Church's director of Adventist-Muslim relations. He frequently presents worship messages to the refugees as they begin their school day. Here he helps two Arabic-speaking students with their Rosetta Stone computer lessons, which supplement the ESL classes.

Another mother with two children arrived as a refugee. She joined the English language school and began her journey to a new future. She is determined to obtain a degree so she can seek a job to support her family. Her husband remains in their homeland awaiting his visa. Today the mother is in her second year of college working toward her goals. She often has told us that coming to the RAP's ESL school was a life-changing experience that she will ever remember.

God tells us in His Holy Word that if we are children of God, it will be evident because of our love. "Dear friends, let us love one another, for love comes from God. Everyone who loves has been born of God and knows God. Whoever does not love does not know God, because God is love" (1John 4:7, 8).

Down just a few more verses is "This is love: not that we loved God, but that he loved us and sent his Son as an atoning sacrifice for our sins. Dear friends, since God so loved us, we also ought to love one another. No one has ever seen God; but if we love one another, God lives in us and his love is made complete in us" (verses 10–12).

This is not an option for the Christian; it is what we will be doing if God is truly living in us. Love will be the active, driving force in our life. Not love just for those who love us, but even beyond that.

Jesus gave us some very specific instructions on how to treat people: "You have heard that it was said, 'Love your neighbor and hate your enemy.' But I tell you, love your enemies and pray

> *Love will be the active, driving force in our life.*

for those who persecute you, that you may be children of your Father in heaven. He causes his sun to rise on the evil and the good, and sends rain on the righteous and the unrighteous. If you love those who love you, what reward will you get? Are not even the tax collectors doing that? And if you greet only your own people, what are you doing more than others? Do not even pagans do that? Be perfect, therefore, as your heavenly Father is perfect" (Matthew 5:43–48).

That is a very high standard! But perfection, or wholeness, is what Jesus calls us to. If we want to be God's children, then God expects us to live and act like His children.

There is only one way we can live like that and truly love our enemies, and that is if God is living in us and living His life through us. This is the ultimate reality of truly partnering with God. We are going to be different from the world around us.

Why is that? It is because we are going to be ruled by love instead of fear. Yes, the world is going to get much worse before Jesus comes. We are going to see a lot of hatred and warfare and evil, but God's love casts out fear.

When we are operating out of fear, we have taken our eyes off Jesus and have forgotten His love for us. Jesus says that if we love only those

Chapter 9   Live

who love us, we are no different than the pagans. God expects much more from us. God expects perfection, or wholeness, and that is possible only when God is living out that wholeness through us.

This is the ultimate reality of living your life in total, complete partnership with God. "For God so loved the world that he gave his one and only Son, that whoever believes in him shall not perish but have eternal life" (John 3:16). Notice that it does not say "For God so loved Christians." It says "For God so loved the world that he gave his one and only Son."

Jesus died for people of every faith, or no faith at all, but most of them don't know it yet. And if we are ever going to get the job done so Christ may return and end all this evil and strife, then we are going to have to love them the same way God loves them.

If we are ever going to get the job done so Christ may return and end all this evil and strife, then we are going to have to love them the same way God loves them.

Jesus tells us exactly what must happen before He can return: "This gospel of the kingdom will be preached in the whole world as a testimony to all nations, and then the end will come" (Matt. 24:14). How is that going to happen if we don't love our neighbors? How are we going to reach the Muslims, Hindus, Buddhists, and atheists if we are not loving and kind to them? Would you listen to someone who hates you? Then why should they?

How can we be turning our backs on the hundreds of thousands who are fleeing from their homelands for fear of their lives? God is bringing them to our neighborhoods so they can have the opportunity to know Him. God loves them. They are His children, and He longs to bring them home to live with Him. It is our opportunity to love and accept them so that they have the opportunity to learn about God and His love for them.

God wants to help us finish the work of spreading the gospel to the entire world because He wants to come and bring an end to this sin-sick world we live in! Don't you want that to happen too? God wants to live through you to accomplish His goal so that He can come soon and take us to our heavenly home. Are you willing to let God use you for His purposes? Are you really ready to partner with Him?

As we have discovered, God is more than willing to provide us with all the necessary resources to accomplish His will and purposes for our life. But we have to be open and willing to allow it to happen. Are you willing to be used by God? What will you do when a Muslim, Hindu, Buddhist, or atheist moves next door to you?

Jesus says of those who will be ready and waiting for His return, "Come, you who are blessed by my Father; take your inheritance, the kingdom prepared for you since the creation of the world. For I was hungry and you gave me something to eat, I was thirsty and you gave me something to drink, I was a stranger and you invited me in, I needed clothes and you clothed me, I was sick and you looked after me, I was in prison and you came to visit me" (Matthew 25:34–36).

The righteous will be surprised, and they will respond: "'Lord, when did we see you hungry and feed you, or thirsty and give you something to drink? When did we see you a stranger and invite you in, or needing clothes and clothe you? When did we see you sick or in prison and go to visit you?'

"The King will reply, 'Truly I tell you, whatever you did for one of the least of these brothers and sisters of mine, you did for me'" (verses 37–40).

Oh, we don't do it to earn eternal life. Jesus has already purchased our eternal life and given it to us as a gift. But we do these things because Jesus is loving others through us. May we be loving, generous, kind Christians as we live together with our God. May those who see us know that we have been with Jesus, and He is living His life through us. The only way we will ever see peace on this earth will be if Christians take the lead and love as God lives in us. There is no other way, because God is the source of all love. We love because He first loved us.

Chapter 10
Abide

Abide in me, and I in you. As the branch cannot bear fruit of itself,

except it abide in the vine; no more can ye, except ye abide in me.

John 15:4, KJV.

Basheija describes herself as having been "a very rich woman" when she and her family lived in the Democratic Republic of the Congo. Their large farm produced coffee beans, bananas, and other vegetables and fruit in abundance. Living in an agrarian society, they were able to grow all that they needed and have plenty to sell at the market.

After the ethnic hostilities in Rwanda spilled over into her country, her husband was murdered. She fled with her five children, ending up in a refugee camp in Rwanda. Eventually she and four of her children were allowed to come to San Diego, where they found love and acceptance in our church as they moved forward with their life.

Basheija took college English classes while working half time at the P. V. Thrift Store (our job-training site). She enjoyed her job as a sales clerk. She loves people and became friends with many of the customers, some of whom asked her to pray with them. While here she experienced the joy of having a new loving, supportive family in her new homeland. She has

Basheija, right, enjoyed her work and learned to speak better English at P. V. Thrift Store. She and her three younger children have moved to another state to join her older son, who moved there to find work. Pictured with her on her last Sabbath at Paradise Valley Church are Claude, Claudine, and Anita.

Chapter 10   Abide

moved to another state now, where she hopes to find work, keep studying English, and eventually become a United States citizen.

Love has become the hallmark of our ministry here in San Diego. The Bible speaks more about love than any other subject, and I believe the reason is that God is the author of all love. God's

> *Love has become the hallmark of our ministry here in San Diego.*

word tells us, "Dear friends, let us love one another, for love comes from God. Everyone who loves has been born of God and knows God. Whoever does not love does not know God, because God is love" (1 John 4:7, 8).

Now, immediately there is a problem. Don't you know people who don't serve God who love? Don't you know people who fall in love with each other but who don't know God? How can the Bible say that "everyone who loves has been born of God and knows God"?

One of the problems is that in the language of the New Testament, there were three distinct words describing different kinds of love, while the English language has only one, so this can get confusing. In Greek there was *phileo* love, which refers to what we could call "friendship" love. If you and I are friends, we share *phileo* love or friendship love for each other.

A second word the Greeks had was *eros,* love from which we get our word "erotic," and this of course is used in the area of romantic love.

But the kind of love spoken of here in our Bible text, and the primary word for love used throughout the Bible is the word *agape.* This is describing a pure, unconditional love. It is a love that is unselfish, not motivated by any physical need or desire. It is a love that is unnatural in that it doesn't ask or require anything in return.

In our human relationships, we are by nature selfish and self-serving. We naturally love *if* we are loved in return. That kind of love is not the pure *agape* love spoken of in the text above. This *agape* kind of unconditional, selfless love is truly so unnatural that we can have it only if, as our text says, "everyone who loves has been born of God and knows God."

But if we are going to be successful in all our relationships, and particularly in living the Christian life, we do need to have this unconditional kind of love. Read further: "This is how God showed his love among us: He sent his one and only Son into the world that we might live through him. This is love: not that we loved God, but that he loved us and sent his Son as an atoning sacrifice for our sins" (verses 9, 10).

God demonstrates for us what this love really looks like by sending His one and only Son down to us to live and ultimately die for us. "You see, at just the right time, when we were still powerless, Christ died for the ungodly. Very rarely will anyone die for a righteous person, though for a good person someone might possibly dare to die. But God demonstrates his own love for us in this: While we were still sinners, Christ died for us" (Romans 5:6–8).

God did not do as we so often do and say, "I will love you … if." Christ came *while we were still sinners, and died for us.* That is what unconditional *agape* love looks like. This love is such a high love that it is impossible to have any other way. You cannot have unconditional *agape* love for your enemies without truly knowing and being connected to God.

Jesus demonstrates how we must relate to everyone, including our enemies. But we can only do this if we are daily abiding in Him and He is living His life through us.

During the past five years, Ephraim has had the joy of seeing the Refugee Assimilation Project reach out to embrace and affirm more and more families. His loving Christian service has motivated and inspired others along the way.

How much different would our lives and world be if we actually lived with this kind of love for those around us? How different would this world be if instead of fighting and bombing those we perceive as our enemies we loved them unconditionally? Could they remain enemies if instead of our fighting back we heaped this kind of unconditional love on them?

How would your life be different at home if, instead of fighting with your spouse or children, you unconditionally loved them as they are, where they are, with no expectations or strings attached? Unconditional love means that there is literally nothing they can do to make you stop loving them. No matter what

Chapter 10   Abide

they say or do, you would die for them instead of hurting them. Do you have that kind of love? No wonder John stated, "Everyone who [unconditionally, *agape*] loves has been born of God and knows God. Whoever does not [unconditionally, *agape*] love does not know God, because God is [*agape*] love" (verses 7, 8).

Reading further: "Dear friends, since God so loved us, we also ought to love one another. No one has ever seen God; but if we love one another, God lives in us and his love is made complete in us" (verses 11, 12). This is what makes a Christian different from everyone else in the world! And this is why John says it is possible to love like this only if we have been born again of God. It is truly a love that is foreign in our world. You don't see this kind of love anywhere else. Unfortunately, you don't see a whole lot of it even in the churches today either, because many who call themselves Christians are not really experiencing this kind of a close relationship with God.

But God is not through! Please keep reading: "This is how we *know* that we live in Him and He in us: He has given us of his Spirit. And we have seen and testify that the Father has sent his Son to be the Savior of the world. If anyone acknowledges that Jesus is the Son of God, God lives in them and they in God. And so we know and rely on the love God has for us. God is love. Whoever lives in love lives in God, and God in them" (verses 13–16).

God is the only source of this kind of love. You can have it in no other way. It can be yours only when you are living in and relying on God's love for you. We can experience this kind of love only when God is living His life through us. This is why the world doesn't have it. This is why there is so much warfare and hatred in our world, because the vast majority of the world is living separated from God.

Calling yourself a Christian does not make you a Christian. Being a Christian means that God is living in you, you are living in His love, and then His love is being lived out through you in the your community. But there's still more. Let's keep reading: "This is how love is made complete among us so that we will have confidence on the day of judgment: In this world we are like Jesus. There is no fear in love. But perfect love drives out fear, because fear has to do with punishment. The one who fears is not made perfect in love.

"We love because he first loved us. Whoever claims to love God yet hates a brother or sister is a liar. For whoever does not love their brother and sister, whom they have seen, cannot love God, whom they have not seen. And he has given us this command: Anyone who loves God must also love their brother and sister" (verses 17–21).

Loving brothers and sisters is not an option. "But oh," I hear you say, "you don't know what they have done to me ..." No, and I don't care what they have done. It is not an option to love or not love. If we are serious about being a Christian, if we really want to live the Christian life, it is not an option. "Anyone who loves God must also love their brother and sister."

Anyone who loves God must also love their brother and sister.

Now, we could get into an argument about who our "brother and sister" are and miss the whole point. We are *all* sons and daughters of God; therefore, we are *all* brothers and sisters through God. I don't care what country you were born in or what language you speak. You are my brother or sister.

If you find yourself hating your brother or sister, *which means hating any other person,* then you have a problem. The problem is not that you hate them; the problem is your relationship with God. Because if you really have the proper relationship with God, you will also have God's unconditional *agape* love in your life. That is what the Bible says. These are not my words, they are God's. Read it again: "Let us love one another, for love comes from God. Everyone who loves has been born of God and knows God. Whoever does not love does not know God, because God is love" (verses 7, 8).

We must remain in the love of God, and with God living in us, may we share God's unconditional *agape* love to a world that is in desperate need of it. Let's make a difference in our home, at our workplace, in our school, and in our world. But first let's make a difference in our own life, and actually abide with Christ. I think Ephraim Bendantunguka, about whom I have written throughout this book, exemplifies abiding with Christ and living in God's love.

A few months ago at our staff meeting Ephraim said that our refugee project had given assistance to more than 100 refugees from his home continent, a major source of satisfaction to him. In addition, Ephraim has cheerfully helped our students from countries as diverse as Bhutan, China, Colombia, Iraq, Afghanistan, and Iran.

He has driven them to appointments, helped them with forms and documents, and moved them into better apartments. I recall him once hauling gallons of water daily for more than a month to a family who had

Chapter 10 Abide

no running water in their apartment, to make sure that they had water to drink and to cook and bathe with. His loving Christian service has given vision and motivation to others, and this whole experience has been life-changing. It certainly has changed mine!

Let's go back once again to the final words of Christ as John records them. Christ and His disciples are walking from that upper room to the Garden of Gethsemane, where Jesus knows He is going to be betrayed at the hands of His friend Judas. He has begun the walk from death row to the cross, where He will pay the ultimate sacrifice for His enemies. His words to His disciples are appropriate for us in our world today: "I am the vine; you are the branches. If you remain in me and I in you, you will bear much fruit; apart from me you can do nothing. If you do not remain in me, you are like a branch that is thrown away and withers; such branches are picked up, thrown into the fire and burned. If you remain in me and my words remain in you, ask whatever you wish, and it will be done for you. This is to my Father's glory, that you bear much fruit, showing yourselves to be my disciples.

"As the Father has loved me, so have I loved you. Now remain in my love" (John 15:5–9).

If we are remaining connected to the Vine, Christ Jesus, then Christ is living His life through us. Life then becomes a process of accepting, obeying, and living in and through Christ Jesus. Without Him we are powerless, but together with Christ, remaining or abiding in Him, there is nothing we cannot accomplish.

This thought sums up this entire book. I hope you also are abiding in Christ and experiencing the power He gives you. Whatever we have accomplished, or will accomplish in the future, is *all* because of what God is doing in and through us as we abide in Him. God is doing great and marvelous things through His children here at the Paradise Valley Church. It is His work, and we are honored and privileged to be His partners to accomplish whatever He asks us to do. This is only the beginning, as we remain faithful to Him, surrendered and abiding.

Come visit us in person, or on our web page, www.FriendshipsForHope.org. We would love to hear from you about how God is working through your life as you abide in Him and allow Him to accomplish His work through His love in your community.

We invite you to visit our web page at: www.FriendshipsForHope.org and watch some of the videos posted there about our work and meet some of our students and hear their stories as we post them there. If God leads you to support our ministry, you can do so on our web page as well.

To God be the glory!

Friendships For Hope

OUR MISSION

We believe we are called to help the oppressed, poor, and refugees of our community to become educationally, economically, physically and socially viable. Friendships For Hope provides the poor and refugees of San Diego County a safe loving environment where they are able to obtain the essential tools to start a new life in our mutual community.

OUR VISION

As we are helping refugees to become self-sufficient it is the goal that our program also find ways to become self-sustaining within the next 10 years (by 2025). We aim to lead by example and practice what we are teaching to the refugees.

Visit our Web page to learn more about our work with the refugee community in San Diego at:
wwwFriendshipsForHope.org

We are a 501(c)(3) Non-profit Charity

A Personal Testimony from One of Our Students*

My husband and I left our country the Democratic republic of Congo in 2004 because of war .we went in Uganda. We started living as refugees , there life wasn't easy because of insecurity. In 2011we thank God because we received a letter from UNHCR saying that we are welcomed in USA . In 2012 we came in USA , we didn't speak any English .A friend directed us to Adventist Church and we met Peggy and her husband Pastor Will James. They welcome us to the church Bible class and to church English class , they keep giving us good, clothes, find jobs for us. We have been working for 2 years and they still helping us like family. We think God for seeing his hands trough Peggy and Pastor Will James. May God bless them for everything they still doing to help refugees. Now we have 3 children and feel good and we continue to pray God for our future. thanks Reheema

*not edited

We invite you to view the complete
selection of titles we publish at:

www.TEACHServices.com

scan with your mobile
device to go directly
to our website

Please write or email us your praises, reactions, or
thoughts about this or any other book we publish at:

11 Quartermaster Circle
Fort Oglethorpe, GA 30742

Info@TEACHServices.com

TEACH Services, Inc., titles may be purchased in bulk for
educational, business, fund-raising, or sales promotional use.
For information, please e-mail:

BulkSales@TEACHServices.com

Finally if you are interested in seeing
your own book in print, please contact us at

publishing@TEACHServices.com

We would be happy to review your manuscript for free.

CPSIA information can be obtained
at www.ICGtesting.com
Printed in the USA
FSOW03n0740151016
26109FS